Landmark Vis

Kefal

Brian & Eileen Anderson

Published by

Landmark Publishing

Ashbourne Hall, Cokayne Ave, Ashbourne,
Derbyshire DE6 1EJ England

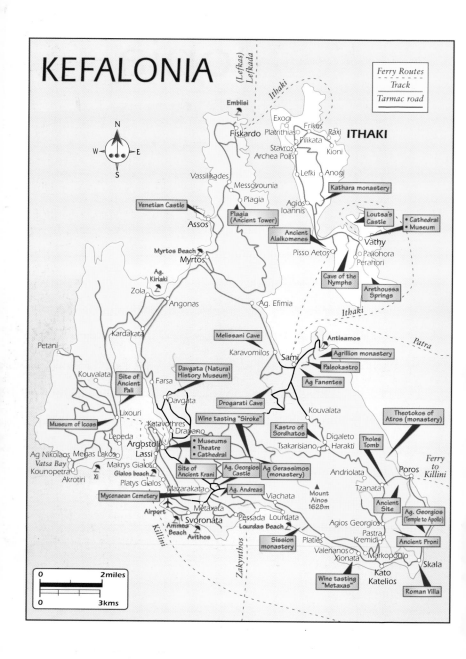

KEFALONIA

Ferry Routes
Track
Tarmac road

N
W — E
S

(Lefkas)
Lefkada

Ithaki

Emblisi

Fiskardo

Exogi
Platrithias
Stavros
Archea Polis
Frikes
Pilikata
Raxi **ITHAKI**
Kioni
Lefki
Anogi

Vassilikades

Messovounia

Plagia

Agios
Ioannis

Kathara monastery

Venetian Castle

Assos

Plagia
(Ancient Tower)

Ancient
Alalkomenes

Loutsa's
Castle

Cathedral
Museum

Vathy

Myrtos Beach
Myrtos

Pisso Aetos

Paliohora
Perahori

Ag.
Kiriaki

Cave of the
Nymphs

Zola

Angonas

Ag. Efimia

Arethoussa
Springs

Ithaki

Patra

Petani

Kardakata

Melissani Cave

Karavomilos

Sami

Antisamos

Agrillion monastery

Paleokastro

Kouvalata

Site of
Ancient
Pali

Farsa

Davgata (Natural
History Museum)

Davgata

Ag Fanentes

Lixouri

Katavorhres
Drapano

Drogarati Cave

Wine tasting "Siroke"

Kastro of
Sordhatos

Kouvalata

Museum of Icoas

Lepeda

Argostoli
Lassi

Tsakarisiano

Digaleto
Harakti

Theotokos of
Atros (monastery)

Ag Nikolaos Megas Lakos
Vatsa Bay
Kounopetra
Akrotiri

Makrys Gialos
Gialos beach
Platys Gialos
Xi

Museums
Theatre
Cathedral

Site of
Ancient Krani

Ag. Georgios
Castle

Ag Gerassimos
(monastery)

Andriolata

Tholes
Tomb

Ferry
to
Killini

Poros

Tzanata

Mycenaean Cemetery

Mazarakata

Ag. Andreas

Viachata

Mount
Ainos
1628m

Ancient
Site

Ag. Georgios
(temple to Apollo)

Airport

Killini

Metaxata

Svoronata

Ammes
Beach
Avithos

Pessada
Lourdata
Lourdas Beach

Agios Georgios

Pastra
Kremidi

Ancient Proni

Sission
monastery

Platies

Valeanos
Xionata

Markopoulo

Skala

Zakynthos

Wine tasting
"Metaxas"

Kato
Katelios

Roman Villa

0   2miles
0   3kms

Opposite page: Ag. Fanen

Kefalonia

Brian & Eileen Anderson

Feature Boxes

LANDMARK HOTSPOTS

Places not to be missed on Kefalonia:

Argostoli
Good waterside atmosphere, delightful main square, pedestrianised shopping, excellent fruit market and museums.

Assos
Scenic position on the neck of a peninsula, natural beauty, intimate atmosphere and Venetian castle.

Fiskardo
Delightful yachting port, atmospheric water front, ancient remains.

Melissani cave
Watery cave explored by boat.

Drogarati cave
Cave to explore on foot.

Myrtos beach
Scenic beach of silver sand.

Lassi and Gialos beaches
Golden sandy beaches, water sports and tourist facilities.

Ithaka
Mountainous island, pretty fishing villages and attractive main town.

Introduction

The half-forgotten island of Cephallonia rises improvidently and inadvisedly from the Ionian sea: it is an island so immense in antiquity that the very rocks themselves exhale nostalgia and the red earth lies stupefied not only by the sun but by the impossible weight of memory

writes Louis de Bernières in Captain Corelli's Mandolin.

No Greek island is quite the same as another no matter how physically close they may lie and Kefalonia stands out as a different experience which has already gathered a following of devotees intent on returning year after year. Scenery makes the first impression, it is so different to the other Ionian islands. Not here the luscious green mantle of Corfu or the pastoral ambience of Zakynthos, instead fir-capped limestone mountains thrust high to meet an achingly blue sky. A jumble of scenic cameos follow one by one around an indented coastline with picturesque headlands, bays, peninsulas, inlets within inlets and beaches of silver and gold.

If nature provides the backcloth, people and culture provide the interest. The tradition of friendliness found throughout the Ionian islands is found in good measure on Kefalonia. Do not expect to see an old way of life on the island. Kefalonia's cultural heritage may well stretch back to Mycenaean times, and there are rich traces still to be seen around the island, but the thread of history is not continuous. A massive earthquake in 1953 proved to be one of those staggering events that totally reset the course of the island. It emerged from total devastation to rebuild from the ruins but old ways, old habits and old customs disappeared with the earthquake only to be reborn in modern ways in new surroundings.

Now the island looks to tourism and its resorts are in the development phase. There is no headlong rush, the path into tourism is being taken quite slowly and it is wrong to think of the island as one great builders' yard. Most of the resorts are comparatively small but all the services are in place to help the visitor make the most of the day but not necessarily of the night. It is a place to relax, to enjoy the beach, catch some sightseeing, delve into Mycenaean history, eat well and feel content.

Kefalonia is really two islands for the price of one. Just a short sail away is Ithaka, another island awaiting exploration. Homeric associations lie around every corner and it is a place to let fantasies run freely while exploring its ports and villages.

LOCATION

Kefalonia, with an area of 266 sq miles (688sq km), is the largest of the seven Ionian islands but with around only 32,000 inhabitants is not the most populous. Lying almost opposite the entrance to the Gulf of Patras, it is located between Lefkas to the north and Zakynthos (Zante) to the south. Mountains dominate the island with the highest peak, Mt Ainos, in the south reaching an altitude of 5,335ft (1,626m) but there are as many as ten peaks topping 2,953ft (900m). Extending out to the west is the extensive Lixouri (Paliki) peninsula enclosing the Gulf of Argostoli. This is less mountainous than the rest of the island and is best described as hilly. Its irregular shape makes quoting dimensions difficult but on a north to south axis it is around 20 miles (32km) long and east to west 16.9 miles (27km) but that also includes the Gulf of Argostoli. All the major settlements are located around the coast with only smaller villages tucked away in the hills.

Livathos plain, just south of Argostoli is one of the largest and most fertile of the island's plains which are few and small. Collectively these plains are sufficient to sustain an important agricultural sector producing olives, grapes, and figs with other fruit and vegetables. Livestock also contributes to the economy and the mountains are used to sustain large herds of goats. Fishing is the other mainstay of the economy with tourism, a growth industry, starting to make an impact.

ON THE ROCKS

Kefalonia consists largely of limestone rock formations in permeable stratas which are not dissimilar to the karst formations seen along the Adriatic coast. Slowly but steadily over aeons of time, rainwater acidified by the carbon dioxide of the atmosphere permeates and dissolves these limestones to generate caverns, caves and swallow holes. Caves the island certainly has and two of these, Drogarati and Melissani caves have become tourist features but equally fascinating are the island's swallow holes.

Swallow Holes

The entrance to the swallow holes lies just north of Argostoli, towards the tip of the peninsula at Katavothres. Sea water disappears down the hole with such force that, in the nineteenth century, an Englishman built a water mill to harness the energy. It was only in 1963 that a team of Austrian geologists, with the aid of 353lb (160kg) of a soluble red dye, were fully able to determine with certainty the path taken by the water. The flow is easterly beneath the island, collecting rainwater percolating through the mountain mass en route. Some of the flow emerges into the lake in Melissani cave whilst the rest discharges into the sea at Karavomilos near Sami.

WHEN TO GO

Easter time in April is about the earliest that can be considered. Even at this time there is a risk that the weather will be cold and showery but, if the sun is shining, the island is at its most beautiful. At this time the sea is still cold but the sun is easily hot enough to burn and sunbathers still need to take care.

Spring is a delightful season when the trees are vivid green and the wild flowers at their very best. Fortunately, the spring flowers extend into May and May is generally more reliable for weather. Daytime temperatures start to rise but the evenings are still cool. It is not always warm enough to dine outside in the evening in the early part of the month but night-time temperatures too are on the rise and it soon becomes possible, well before the month is out. The island has plenty of visitors in these early months but not enough to make it busy with the result that, although bars and tavernas are usually in full swing, some of the water sports have not yet opened.

Things warm up in June in every sense. The days and nights get hotter and the island tourist machine moves into top gear. Nowhere is too crowded and independent visitors can still expect to find accommodation without too much trouble, except in the Lassi area which is fully booked to tour operators. All that changes in July, with the Greeks and Italians moving into their holiday season, and the island suddenly becomes very crowded. July and August are the hottest months of the year and the least comfortable on the island. Beaches are full and the facilities often at full stretch.

Even the locals welcome September when the crowds have departed and some of the intense heat leaves the sun. Many regard September as the best month of the summer with the sea still warm and the sun still pouring incessantly from the sky although the autumn rains may well start before the month is out. October is cooler with more cloudy and rainy days but still with fine, sunny periods.

PEOPLE AND CULTURE

In spite of the island's turbulent history and a parade of different masters over the centuries, the people of Kefalonia have retained their own brand of the Greek character. This character, tempered by western influences, from the Venetians, the French and the British, over the centuries, is a little different from that observed in the more easterly parts but the language and the church provided a continuity which has kept the people in touch with their own identity.

Hospitable people

Their conviviality and hospitality to strangers wins the island many friends. Sadly, these qualities are subdued by the pressure of work in the height of the tourist season but never squashed. Away from all the bustle, it takes only a cheerful greeting, sometimes only a smile, to be on the receiving end of their hospitality. It may take the form of an orange pulled from a bag or a handful of freshly grown broad beans but whatever it is, it is considered bad manners to refuse. Language barriers don't exist for the Greeks and mostly they will chatter away in their native tongue in the full expectancy that you will understand some or part of whatever they are saying. Body language and gesticulations play a full part too.

MAINLAND AND ISLAND HOPPING

Kefalonia makes a very convenient base for a two centre holiday but it needs a little planning beforehand. With prior permission from the car hire company, it is very easy to escape by ferry from **Argostoli or** Poros over to Killini in the Peloponnese which instantly opens up a whole new range of possibilities. **Alternatively, there are flights connecting the Ionian Islands which is specially convenient for reaching Corfu. Here are a few suggestions for ferry excursions;**

Strike south for Olympia, easily reached within the first day, and then on to explore the Mani, the southern central peninsula of the Peloponnese. Mani, a wild and rugged refuge for fugitives in the past, is friendly enough now but the hints of hostility in the castle-like tower houses and the terrain makes this a place apart in Greece. The ruins of **Monemvasia** medieval Mistra are not that far away and could be incorporated into the return journey.

Using a northern route, Corinth and the Argolid are great places to visit. En route there is a great little rack and pinion railway to try out, from Diakopto on the coast to the mountain village of Kalavrita. The Argolid, stronghold of the Mycenaeans, has an abundance of ancient sites to explore including Mycenae itself and Ancient Corinth. Nafplio or nearby Tolon are ideal bases for exploring this region.

A trip to Delphi is easily accomplished within the day although a one or two night stop is recommended to leave time to absorb and enjoy the site of the ancient oracle. The route from Killini is to head north and cross **the bridge** to the northern mainland at Rio. From Andirio it is basically a coastal run east to Itea then a short leg inland to Delphi.

Two neighbouring Ionian islands, Lefkas and **Zakynthos (Zante)**, are within easy reach of Kefalonia. Fiskardo and Sami have daily ferry services to Lefkas. Fiskardo ferries serve both Vasiliki, in the south, and Nidri on the east coast while Sami ferries call in at Ithaka on the way.

For **Zakynthos (Zante)**, ferries leave from Pessada, reached via Peratata, and dock at Ag Nikolaos at the northern tip of the island.

One of the most convenient ways to see the neighbouring island and Olympia on the mainland is to join an organised tour. Check the tours offered by the KTEL bus service.

For further details of **Zakynthos (Zante)**, see the Landmark guide.

Above left: Moni Ag. Agrilion
Above right: Ag. Efimia
Right: Skala Beach
Below: Sami

The trouble with 'g'

Many visitors experience considerable difficulties with the Greek alphabet and language. Even though many signs are transliterated into the Latin alphabet, it is still not easy to get the pronunciation correct without understanding some of the basic rules. The letter g is one that seems to cause most problems, mainly because it crops up in one frequently used word, *Agios*, meaning saint, which is used in many church and place names.

The rules of pronunciation for this letter are quite simple. If g is followed by e or i it is pronounced as a **y**, otherwise it remains **g**. So *Platys Gialos* is pronounced *Platys Yialos* and the word for a saint, *Agios*, pronounced *Ayios* (or *Ayia* for a lady).

11

The family unit is strong and still the basis of Greek society, although there are signs that the bonds are starting to weaken under western influences. It is sons who receive the adulation and are totally spoilt by their parents. This does not mean that daughters are not welcomed, as in some societies, and the ideal family is regarded as one son and one daughter.

Parental influence is still strong when the time is right for their children to marry. Arranged marriages have not entirely disappeared. They are no longer the norm but parents still have a dominant role in satisfying the demands of society and tradition. It is the duty of the son to stand by his parents to ensure that suitable matches are made for all his sisters before he can contemplate marriage. Although a dowry is no longer a legal requirement, a law only recently repealed, it is still perpetuated. A girl goes into marriage often with the gift of a furnished house or apartment from her parents. It remains the girl's property and her security. In the same way gifts of gold to the bride, also to provide for her security, are not unusual. At least the newly wedded couple start life without the burden of debt and are able to build and plan a future for their own children.

The family unit extends into business too. The Greek preference is for self employment or failing that a secure job with the state. Most small businesses employ only family and are eventually passed down via sons and daughters.

It is still a male dominated society but attitudes are slowly changing amongst the younger generation. Just a short time ago, only young men had the freedom to go out alone but this too has changed and young women are now part of the social scene. The role of women in the broader society has been recognized in legislation. They acquired the vote only in 1952 and the first woman Deputy was elected to Parliament the following year.

Sexual discrimination in career opportunities and in the place of work has been outlawed. Many practical steps have been taken to assist the integration of women as equals in society. Low cost nurseries offering child places have been provided to free women to work and women have acquired rights of ownership after marriage and an equal share of communal property on divorce. Women now hold important posts in all branches of the Civil Service and in commerce but, in spite of all their progress, equality is only accepted in the big cities. Throughout rural Greece it remains contrary to the culture and fundamental change will only be fully accepted very slowly.

For women touring alone in Greece there are no exceptional problems. The incidence of violent crime, including rape, is much lower than in other western societies. But it is not unknown and the same wariness of the possible situations should be observed, especially in a large city. Greek men firmly believe they are irresistible to all women so their attentions can be expected.

ARTS

One legacy of the Venetian rule is music, which has remained strong on Kefalonia. Argostoli has a well-attended Philharmonic School for the teaching of wind and brass instruments and concerts are held from time to time. Lixouri too has a Philharmonic Society and most larger towns and villages have their own bands.

Greek dancing is popular on the island and is very often the highlight of the entertainment at a religious festival. In tourist resorts local dancers often perform in restaurants and tavernas throughout the season. Many of the dances are local to Kefalonia and these show distinct Cretan and Peloponnesian influences arising from historical connections. In addition, entertainments usually include the more popular dances performed throughout the country.

FOOD AND DRINK

Watching the Greeks eat is a pleasure in itself. Seldom do they order individually, instead they order a vast number of communal dishes which fill the table to overflowing. They are far less concerned about cold food and many dishes that arrive hot are cold before they are eaten. Some tourists find it a bit disconcerting when their meals are actually served on the cool side but, in most areas, the message that tourists generally like their food hot has registered.

Although the Greek cuisine is quite extensive, tavernas tend only to have a limited menu. Lunch time, between two and three o'clock after work finishes, is the only meal of the day for which the chef will prepare a range of cooked dishes. For the evening trade, and the Greeks are notoriously late eaters, the menu offers whatever is left over from lunch, which has often been kept warm for hours, and a range of grills which are cooked to order.

Charcoal is generally used for grilling and it is not unusual to see large charcoal grills by the doorway or outside in summer. Although the tavernas are the traditional eating places, Argostoli town and main resorts have a selection of restaurants that provide a better standard of decor in particular and offer a more international cuisine (see feature box – Eating out in Argostoli, p39).

MEZEDES

Menus usually offer a range of small dishes, known as *mezedes*, for starters. These include *tzatziki* (a yoghurt, cucumber and garlic dip), taramasalata (fish roe mixed with potato, oil and vinegar), *melitzano salata* (an aubergine dip with tomato and garlic) and humus, another dip this time from chick-peas. Fresh vegetables are rarely available but two vegetables that turn up as mezedes are gigantes (butter beans cooked in tomato and oil) and peas (*arakas*). *Saganaki*, fried cheese, is another interesting starter. The waiter will raise an eyebrow if *mezedes* are ordered separately by each individual, even tourists are expected to order a selection and share in Greek style.

Salads may be preferred as starters or as part of the starters and the most popular is the village salad or *horiatiki salata* which may include lettuce, or cabbage, but less so now, tomato, onion, cucumber, feta cheese and olives. Tomatoes, cucumber, feta cheese and lettuce (*maruli*) are also offered as separate dishes.

MAIN COURSE

Ready cooked dishes may include the familiar moussaka, a mince dish with aubergines, potato and béchamel sauce, veal in tomato (*kokanisto*), *stifado* (veal stew with

FAST FOOD GREEK STYLE

The Greeks are great nibblers, particularly in the mornings, so there is no shortage of fast-food.

'Pies' (*pitta*) with various fillings, usually made with filo pastry and looking like a Cornish pasty:

- *Tiropitta*: cheese. This is the most universally popular and found every where.
- *Spanakopitta*: spinach only or with cheese and eggs.
- *Kreatopitta*: minced meat.
- *Pizza*: usually take-away small ones or sometimes sold as pieces.

and for the sweet tooth:

- *Milopitta*: apple.
- *Bougatza*: vanilla custard.
- *Souvlaki*: small pieces of meat on a wooden skewer served with a lump of bread or with pitta.
- *Doner me pitta*: slices of meat from the gyros (meat cooked on a vertical spit) placed in a pitta parcel with a little yoghurt, tomato and onion.
- *Tost*: usually a slice of ham and cheese toasted between bread.

Freshly pressed orange juice is widely available.

Eating out, Poros

Above & left: Assos

onions) or *yiovetsi* (oven cooked lamb served with pasta). Chicken cooked on the spit is popular and inexpensive but first amongst the grills is *souvlaki*, veal or pork on a skewer. Chops, pork, lamb or veal, are ever present on the evening menus as are *keftedes* (spicy meat balls) and *biftekia* (mince burgers). Kefalonian specialities include *kouneli* (rabbit), *sofrito*, veal cooked in wine with herbs, garlic and vinegar and served with a thick sauce and Kefalonian meat pie which has a tasty filling of meat and rice.

Fish is sometimes on offer but for a selection it is better to find a fish taverna, *psaria taverna*. Fish is becoming increasingly expensive and prices on the menu are often expressed per kilogram, which makes them look sky high. In practice, a fish is weighed off and the charge is for that weight. A typical portion is around 14oz (400gm). Lobster (*astakos*) and red mullet (*barbounia*) are usually top of the menu and are expensive as are shrimps (*garides*). Octopus, grilled or cooked in wine is less expensive as is squid (*kalamari*). At the cheap end is the small whitebait (*marides*), which is eaten in its entirety, head and all. This dish is often available as a starter in a fish restaurant. Desserts are very limited, usually fruit, but the popularity of yoghurt and honey, and crème caramel, amongst tourists is now recognized. If you have tucked into your meal with obvious enjoyment, the proprietor may produce a plate of fruit, peeled and presented with his compliments.

DRINKS

Some Greeks prefer to drink ouzo with meals and this is served in small bottles and usually taken with water. Others choose retsina, a resinated wine, which is an acquired taste and the usual commercial brand is Kourtaki although the less resinated Melamatina or Liokari are better. Most wine lists contain some of the country's acknowledged good wines like Boutari Naoussa and Lac des Roches as well as some medium priced popular ones like Kambas, Rotonda and Domestica. Kefalonia has plenty of vines and a number of wine manufacturers but locals still make their own which is usually good and much cheaper than the branded labels. Ask for *krasi dopio* (local wine) or *spitiko krasi* (house wine) which is usually served in a carafe or metal jug.

FLORA AND FAUNA

Flowers abound in spring from the ubiquitous Spanish broom to rare wild orchids but the best time to see them is from late March through April into May, although the season persists longer around the top of Mount Ainos. This latter area is now protected as National Park and one of the species it seeks to protect is the endemic fir tree, *Abies cephalonia*.

Orchids are prominent amongst the spring flora and some thirty-one different species have been recorded so far and there are probably still more to find. Despite the heat and the lack of water in summer, there are always a few flowers to be seen, like the beautiful sea daffodil, *Pancratium maritimum*, and the mulleins. Autumn rains bring out the crocus and cyclamen in a new flush of flowers that help to keep winter bright until spring gets into its stride once again.

The fauna is surprisingly good too and the island has a wide range of wild animals including foxes, hares, weasels, pine martens and hedgehogs. Wild horses, descended from abandoned horses, still exist on Mt Ainos but are a threatened species. Tortoises are around in great numbers and these too are often seen on the road. Greek drivers believe it unlucky to run over a tortoise so they go to great lengths to avoid them.

Snakes are around too in numbers but mostly harmless. Vipers are known to exist but are unlikely to be encountered.

The Natural History Museum of Kefalonia and Ithaka is located in the village of Davgata, a little way north of Argostoli.

Holiday Reading

There is no greater pleasure than reading a book in the location where the book is set and Kefalonia has two great treats in store. One is a modern classic, *Captain Corelli's Mandolin* by Louis Bernières, and the other a very ancient classic, none other than *Homer's Odyssey*. Both have powerful connections with the island and more recently *Captain Corelli's Mandolin* was filmed on the island (see also page 61 for feature box on *Captain Corelli's Mandolin*).

HISTORY

The island is particularly rich in prehistoric remains. Significant finds of stone axe-heads, cleavers and arrow-heads have been made at a number of locations including Sami,

THE KEFALONIAN FIR

There was a time when Mount Ainos was heavily forested with *Abies cephalonia*, the Kefalonian fir, which grows above altitudes of around 2,625ft (800m). In mass the trees look very dark which led the Venetians to call this range Monte Nero, the black mountain. Forest still exists today but much ravaged by timber demands and repeated fires.

This tree is endemic to the area, not just to the island, and is also found on high ground in much of the southern mainland of Greece. It is a much-prized wood and was in demand as soon as man started building wooden ships. The columns at Knossos in Crete were made from Kefalonian fir and it is very possible that the source was this island. Kefalonia had a thriving Mycenean population at that time which was possibly trading with the Minoans on Crete. Throughout the ages a thriving lumber trade built up largely because Kefalonia's fir forests were accessible and close to the sea for shipping away. In later years the island's forest supplied boatyards in Corfu and Italy.

Forest fires have also played a significant part over the centuries. In 1590 a great part of the forest was lost to fires but over the centuries it regenerated only to suffer an even worse fire in 1797.

In 1962 the area was declared National Park in order to protect this species of fir of which the island is rightly proud.

Fiskardo and the Argostoli peninsula. Although scientific dating is difficult on this type of artifact, they are thought to have arisen around 4000BC and some scholars put them even earlier. Some of these finds are displayed in the Archaeological museum in Argostoli.

THE MYCENAEANS

Organized civilization, which reached a high degree of sophistication, appeared with the Mycenaeans in 1400-1100BC. Kefalonia and nearby Ithaka were clearly preferred locations for the Mycenaeans since there is nothing comparable on any of the other Ionian islands. Settlements were spread around Kefalonia at Krani, near Argostoli, Pali near Lixouri, Sami and Proni, between Skala and Poros. Since the Mycenaeans built in a robust style with huge blocks of stone, remains of their strongholds have survived pilfering and earthquakes and are still to be seen at Krani and Sami as well as impressive tombs at Mazarakata and near Poros. On Ithaka too there was a major settlement at Alalkomenes.

EMERGENCE OF CITY STATES

The Mycenaean period ended around 1100BC when the Dorians

Continued on page 20...

Far left: Campanula versicolor

Left: Wild orchid, Ophrys tenthredinifera

Middle: View from Mount Ainos

Bottom: White Rocks

Opposite page: Assos

invaded from the north wielding superior weapons of iron and Greece entered the Dark Age. Little is known of events on Kefalonia until around the fifth century BC when it appears that some form of democracy emerged paralleling events in mainland Greece.

By this time four city states existed, based on the old Mycenaean fortified settlements. Each pursued its own policies and there was no united front during the Peloponnesian War (431-404 BC) with support divided between Athens and Corinth. Athens settled the issue by taking the island without resistance and using it as a base of operations. Throughout the fourth century BC there was a greater inclination for co-operation between cities throughout the whole of Greece. In this period the Aetolian League formed, which eventually all four Kefalonian cities joined. In this period, along with Zakinthos, they were happily engaged in piracy, taking riches from the Achaeans (Peloponnese) and their allies.

Around 255BC the Achaeans formed their own league that soon grew into a union of the whole of the Peloponnese. Not too pleased with the constant attentions of the raiders from the Aetolian League, the Achaeans called on King Philip V of Macedonia for assistance. Recognizing the strategic importance of Kefalonia, he mounted his first attack against Proni in 218BC but switched to Pali, the most important city on the island at that time. Despite various strategies and attempts, the Macedonians failed.

Meanwhile, Rome and Carthage were at war again in the Second Punic War, which lasted from 218-202BC, during which Philip V of Macedonia allied himself with the Carthaginian general Hannibal. Rome emerged victorious and when asked for help by the eastern Mediterranean Greeks against Philip, the Romans readily agreed and easily defeated him. The Roman colonization of Greece had started.

The Roman Period

Around 189BC, the Romans arrived to take control of Kefalonia and while the other cities capitulated, Sami decided on closing its gates and defending against the aggressor. After a siege lasting four months Sami was forced to surrender and the Romans promptly turned Kefalonia into a naval base from which they could command the seas around western Greece. The prosperity that the island had earlier enjoyed waned during the Roman occupation. In AD337, the Roman Empire had grown so large that it was decided to divide it into two and Kefalonia was included in the eastern section which later became Byzantium.

THE BYZANTINE PERIOD (AD337-1267)

From the fifth to the seventh centuries, Barbarian tribes from Europe, namely the Vandals and Goths were mounting piratical raids against the Roman Empire. Kefalonia, like other Ionian islands, suffered at their hands as well as from the North African Saracens who also mounted raids. Emperor Heraclius reorganized the administrative themes from 629 to 634, to create smaller units more able to organize against these attacks. Kefalonia became head of the Theme of Lombardy and was able to use the combined naval force to defend against the Arab raids. Just as the island was regaining some of her old power and prestige, further changes early in the ninth century demoted the island and divided the theme. Fortunes were restored in 887 when Kefalonia again became the administrative head of the Ionian islands and it held this position for the next 300 years.

By the eleventh century, events and changes in Europe were posing new threats from the Normans who were pushing into this part of the world. In 1081 the Normans, under Robert Guiscard, took Corfu and his son continued south to capture Kefalonia but failed to overcome the resistance of the islanders. Within three years the Byzantines, backed by a now powerful Venice, were able to recover Corfu and dispel the Norman threat from the region. In return Venice was granted certain trading privileges in the region.

There was no lasting peace for the island was again attacked by the Normans and the Genoese. After taking the island in 1147, the Normans were driven out by the Byzantine Emperor Manuel with the help of the Venetians but the island was handed back to the Normans as part of a deal for a peace in 1185. The former corsair, Admiral Margaritus, took control of Kefalonia, Ithaka and Zakynthos and set up his headquarters in St George's Castle on Kefalonia.

THE ORSINI FAMILY (1194-1357)

He was succeeded by Matthios Orsini in 1194 who abolished the Greek orthodox church for Catholicism to gain popularity with the pope. The Byzantine Empire finally crumbled as a result of the Fourth Crusade (1202-4). Thanks to help offered to the Crusades, the Venetians gained control of a number of territories along its trade route to the Levant, which included the Ionian islands, although they did not gain immediate control.

Orsini, once a pirate himself, was nothing if not cunning. By 1209 he decided it was in his best interests to change sides so he declared servitude to the Venetians and pacified the Vatican with the promise of a yearly tribute.

In 1258 he was succeeded by his son, Ricardo, but he was no less devious than his father. With the growing power of Theodore Angelos Comnenos, Despot of Epirus, Ricardo took steps to guard his own interests by marrying his son, Ioannes, to Comnenos' daughter. Ioannes Orsini, cast in the same mould, took control on his father's death. Murder and intrigue within the family followed but the Orsinis held on to power up until 1357. In the final years, Ioannes II, who had murdered his brother, renounced the Orsini lineage and adopted the name Ioannes Angelos Comnenos to court popularity. His most serious mistake was to usurp his sister's dowry, the property of her husband, William Tocco, which was half the island of Zante.

THE TOCCO DYNASTY (1357-1479)

In 1335 Ioannes Angelos Comnenos was poisoned by his wife. In 1357, the King of Naples gave the islands of Kefalonia, Ithaka and Lefkada to Leonard I Tocco. After years of Orsini rule and high taxation, Kefalonia was in a poor state but Leonard adopted a softer policy to advance the welfare and prosperity of the island. This policy survived only as long as Leonard for his successor, Carlo I, already holding land in Epirus, proved to be a greedy and violent ruler until his death in 1429. By this time Venice was engaged in constant running battles with the Turks who were advancing into mainland Greece. Under pressure from the Turks, Carlo II ceded the town of Ioannina to them but they were not appeased and, in 1442, the Turks took control of Zante.

In 1448, Leonard III came to power, the last in a line of five successive Tocco rulers. It was he who

Karavomilos

restored the rights of the Greek Orthodox church and he also who was forced to yield Kefalonia to the Turks in 1484. The Turks conquered and plundered Kefalonia but their period of rule was short, lasting only until the year 1500.

VENETIAN RULE (1500-1797)

Backed by Spain, Venice launched an attack on Kefalonia in 1500 to dispel the Turks. They laid siege to the castle of St George, captured it and slaughtered the Turkish garrison. The Venetians were welcomed as liberators by the inhabitants but they merely exchanged one master for another. Rule was invested in noblemen, who sought to strengthen the island by encouraging immigrants, a policy fully supported by Venice. In this way the population multiplied, farms organized and a merchant fleet developed for trade. Records show that the population grew from 14,000 in 1548 to around 70,000 in 1655. There were many beneficial aspects of the Venetian rule, they introduced grapes for raisin production, for example, which became a major export product, and introduced art and music generally raising the level of civilization.

Troubled times still existed, especially in 1537 when Suleiman the Magnificent declared war on Venice. Kefalonia suffered at the hands of Barbarossa, one time pirate, then admiral of the Turkish fleet, and again after peace had been concluded in 1540. Ali Pasha too attacked Sami in 1571 inflicting considerable damage but avoiding attacking St George's castle, the capital of the island.

Venice, a great power throughout this period, was by the start of the

Above: Assos
Main photograph: Poros

eighteenth century heading into decline. The class system of rule introduced by the Venetians brought its own problems on Kefalonia. Powerful noble families attracted bands of followers, which created trouble, erupting into civil war in 1755 involving the Metaxa and the Anninos families. Venice was powerless to intervene and Kefalonia was ready to court a new protector.

Exhausted by its long struggles, Venice was finally defeated by Napoleon in 1797 and Kefalonia, like the other Ionian islands became a French possession.

FRENCH AND RUSSIAN MASTERS (1797-1809)

The French were greeted with excitement and they responded by outlawing the now hated aristocratic system of rule. In the following year, disaster overtook the French fleet at the Battle of Abukir, after which they were forced to yield the Ionian islands to the Russians and the Turks.

First action of the Russo-Turkish regime was to restore the aristocratic system of administration. In a joint declaration by the Russian and Turkish admirals, the Ionian islands were joined to become one nation, the Septinsular Republic. Fourteen delegates made up the governing senate and eventually a constitution was drawn up which acknowledged

the fact that the Republic was a Russian protectorate.

By the treaty of Tilsit, in 1807, the Ionian islands were ceded back to France who were again greeted warmly. Once again the French occupation was doomed to be short lived but this time the threat came from Britain.

BRITISH RULE (1809-1864)

In 1809, Britain mounted a blockade of the Ionian islands as part of the war against Napoleon and, on 19 September of the same year, hoisted the British flag over Zante castle. Kefalonia and Ithaka quickly surrendered and the British installed provisional governments. The Treaty of Paris in 1815 recognized the United States of the Ionian islands and decreed that it become a British protectorate. Colonel Charles Philippe de Bosset, a Swiss serving in the British army, became provisional governor between 1810 and 1814. During those years he was credited with many public works including the Drapano causeway bridge at Argostoli.

Thomas Maitland, the first Lord High Commissioner in 1815, devised a constitution for the Ionians that concentrated power in his own hands. Although he initiated many public works to improve the infrastructure and protect and encourage

Earthquakes

The seventeenth century saw the start of a series of earthquakes far worse than the island had previously known. An earthquake in 1634 caused great structural damage and took 540 lives and it was the turn of Lixouri to take the brunt of the 1658 quake.

Name that Church

The countryside sometimes seems littered with small, mostly white churches. No matter how simple, each one has a name which can be worked out from the icons contained within. It is fun to try and challenging even with these guidelines. Knowing the Greek alphabet helps for identifying the saints but when ancient script is used, it can be even more difficult.

If the doorway in the iconostasis is central, then the icon of the Virgin Mary should be on the left and the icon of the saint after which the church is named to the left of the Virgin Mary. Christ is on the right of the doorway and St John the Baptist to the right of Christ.

If there is an additional doorway it is usually on the left taking up the space normally reserved for the icon dedicated to the saint of the church. Now, the icon of the saint to which the church is dedicated is then placed on the right of Christ.

It works most of the time but there are still pitfalls to watch out for, especially when the church is dedicated to two or more saints.

---

trade, he was disliked for his autocratic ways. Resistance groups started to form although much of their energy in the early years was directed to supporting the Greeks in their revolution against the Turks.

By 1848 the resistance movement was gaining strength and turning against the British. There were skirmishes with the British army in Argostoli and Lixouri, which led to some relaxation of the laws, including a greater freedom for the press. Union with Greece was now a declared aim and, by 1850, a growing restlessness resulted in still more skirmishes which were put down with violence. Kefalonia, along with the other Ionian islands, were ceded to Greece as a gesture of goodwill when the British backed Prince William of Denmark who became King George I of the Hellenes.

The period of British rule had many positive aspects. Many of the island's roads were constructed, a new Ionian Academy formed, educational standards improved and greater prosperity enjoyed.

UNION WITH GREECE (1864)

After union, Kefalonians had greater freedom of movement and, with repeated earthquakes around the middle of the century, a great wave of emigration commenced to other Greek cities or to other countries. Farming decreased on the island but shipping remained important. Trade unionism appeared in the early decades after union with Greece and political movements started, particularly Socialism.

RESORT GUIDE

Holiday brochures try to make each and every resort sound attractive without always revealing too much about its character. This guide offers a quick outline of the main resorts on the island to help in making the most suitable choice. A more detailed description of the resorts may be found in the main text and those marked with an asterisk are also featured in part 2, the Good Beach Guide. Water sport facilities are indicated by symbols. One # indicates very limited facilities, perhaps just pedaloes or simply boats for hire, while the maximum three indicates the whole gamut from paragliding, jet skis and banana rides down to the less energetic pursuits but remember, full facilities are not always available early and late in the season. Night life has barely developed on the island and is fairly low key.

Starting from Argostoli, the resorts are presented in anti clockwise order around the island.

Argostoli

Argostoli: as the capital town it seems dedicated to pleasure and relaxation. It may not have a resort atmosphere but it has a lot going for it: an interesting waterfront, probably the best eating on the island, some nightlife and it is the hub of the bus network. The main square is the place to see and be seen in the evening. There is no immediate beach but Lassi with its beaches is but a short taxi ride away.

Lassi

Lassi*: lying fairly close to Argostoli, this is perhaps the major resort area on the island. It has a number of fine, sandy beaches, which is its biggest asset but, as a resort, it lacks character. Much of the development, shops, restaurants and accommodation, straggles along the busy main road leading to the airport. ###

Svoronata

Svoronata: small resort almost adjacent to the airport although Kefalonia is not the busiest airport in Greece. Consists largely of accommodation and the sandy beach of Ammes.

Lourdas Beach

Lourdas Beach*: unspoilt resort with a long stretch of sandy beach. Rather isolated with the nearest village, Lourdata considerably uphill and the main road still higher. #

Kato Katelios

Kato Katelios: a small, sleepy resort in the south of the island developing around a fishing port. Good atmosphere with tavernas on hand, expect far more sand than people. #

Skala

Skala*: Scenically situated at the foot of the mountains, the village sits on a pine-clad headland. Large enough to have some life with a good selection of tavernas, cafés and shops along the main street. Good beach of mainly sand. Isolated from the point of view of visiting other places on the island. ##

Poros

Poros: although not large by any means, Poros is one of the bigger resorts on the island, attractive and compact in the middle. Handy for the ferry to Killini and Lefkas. The beach is narrow and mainly shingle. Like Skala above, it is not the best base for touring the island. ###

Sami

Sami: developed around a natural bay, waterfront Sami has a surpris-ingly modern air. It is fairly quiet in the day as visitors walk out either to the shingle beach to the north or make the trek (1.9 miles/ 3km) over the hill to the beautiful Antisamos beach*. #

Fiskardo

Fiskardo: picturesque fishing village and yachting place on the northern tip of the island. Great ambience with a headland to explore and a small, shingle beach close by. #

Assos

Assos: natural beauty spot on the neck of a peninsula. Only a small village with a good, relaxing atmosphere; nearest beach is Myrtos.

Lixouri

Lixouri: located on the Paliki Peninsula almost opposite Argostoli. This is the second largest town on the island and dedicated more to work than pleasure but with a good Greek atmosphere. Ferries run non-stop between here and Argostoli. There is no beach immediately on hand but Lepeda beach* is a thirty-minute walk or a brief taxi ride to the south.

Out and About
Part 2: Good Beach Guide

GOOD BEACH GUIDE

A day out on a different beach provides a refreshing change and the purpose of this guide is to help with choices. Good beaches are never very far away on Kefalonia but this is not intended to be a comprehensive list. It includes only those beaches with good features that reward the effort of getting there. Sandy beaches are selected in the main but outstandingly good shingle beaches are also included. Refer to the map of the island for locations and for ease of reference they are listed in anti-clockwise order starting from Argostoli. Further details may be found by consulting the car tours.

Lassi

Lassi: this is the name given to the peninsula which encloses Argostoli bay but since the development of tourism the area of Lassi seems to have expanded to encompass much of the coastline running southwards towards the airport. The following four beaches which lie close together are now promoted as Lassi.

Kalamia beach

Kalamia beach: the most northerly of the Lassi beaches, part way up the headland. It has a narrow stretch of sand with a band of fine shingle at the water's edge and is set in a small, picturesque bay bounded by white cliffs to the south. Access is by foot, from the road down a track. Facilities include beach beds, umbrellas and a small bar.

Gradakia beach

Gradakia beach: small but deep inlet with sand and a clear sea. Beach beds, umbrellas and a bar provide all the facilities necessary.

Makrys Gialos

Makrys Gialos: situated a short walk down from the main road, this is probably the most popular beach along this coast. A fine, long stretch of golden sand although without great depth. Plenty of facilities including beach furniture, bars, tavernas and a range of water sports; good for families.

Platys Gialos

Platys Gialos: Same character and sand quality as Makrys Gialos but smaller. It has similar facilities but includes changing rooms and showers; also good for families. The inviting spit of sand running out to a small, rocky headland just to the south, known as Tourkopodaro, is part of the White Rocks Hotel complex.

Lourdas beach

Lourdas beach: unless resident in the area, this one is not easy to reach without a car. A long stretch of fine, silver sand with just a little shingle enclosed by a wide bay. There is very little development around so the beach tends to be quiet but there are tavernas to hand and some beach furniture; limited water sports.

Skala

Skala: Good sandy beach that is both long and deep, unlikely to get too crowded. Plenty of facilities to hand, water sports and good for families.

Poros

Poros: not the best beach, mainly shingle and quite narrow, but one of the liveliest for water sports with a whole gamut of activities available from pedaloes to paragliding. Good facilities close on hand.

Antisamos

Antisamos: located 1.9 miles (3km) south of Sami. A sweep of white pebbles lapped by a violet sea in picturesque setting. Beautiful beach, clear waters but minimal facilities, just sun beds, umbrellas and drinks.

Myrtos beach

Myrtos beach: Spectacular beach of fine white sand and shingle nestling into steep cliffs. It is a real sun trap and gets very hot. Accessed from the main road, high above, by a surfaced road. Facilities limited to a beach bar offering sun beds and umbrellas.

Petani

Petani: at the northern end of the Paliki peninsula. An idyllic setting not unlike Myrtos, fine shingle, clear waters and refreshments on hand.

Lixouri

Lepeda beach: located just south of Lixouri, this small cove has a beach of golden sand. Attractive setting and is complete with all the essential facilities.

33

A DAY OUT IN ARGOSTOLI

A stroll around Argostoli will easily fill half a day, including visits to the museums. The large main square is a magnet for the evening *volta* when locals and visitors alike mingle to socialize and watch the world go by. Oleanders add vibrant touches to the streets in summer where shaded outdoor cafés provide cooling drinks. Most of the main points of interest are close to the heart of the town but the lighthouse lies a mile and a quarter (2km) out of town along the peninsula.

The main points of interest in Argostoli are:

- The Archaeological Museum
- Korgialenios History and Folklore Museum
- Central Square
- Lithostroto pedestrianised shopping street
- Fruit and vegetable market
- Fish sellers along the quayside
- Drapano Bridge
- Katavothres swallow holes and the lighthouse of Ag Theodori

Argostoli sits in the shelter of the **Koutavos lagoon**, a natural haven within the larger Gulf of Argostoli. The town itself lies along the peninsula that separates the lagoon from the gulf and is sheltered from sight of the open sea by a chain of low hills. Once the port for Mycenaean Krani, whose remains are scattered in the hills to the east of Argostoli, it later provided anchorage for Saracens and pirates who regularly raided the island.

HISTORY OF THE TOWN

By the time links with the Byzantine empire were broken and the island passed to Venetian control in 1204, it was under the iron grip of the Orsini family. The capital of Kefalonia had already been moved from Pali (near Lixouri) to the castle of St George, 3 miles (5km) south of present day Argostoli. A combination of administrative movement between the Ionian islands and further afield plus a growing trade in raisins brought an increase in shipping to the port. This increased traffic led, in 1560, to a basic dock being built where present day Argostoli stands; then no more than a clutch of fishermen's cottages.

Administrative control remained in the castle though, whilst commercial activity developed apace in the area of the port, a situation that hampered the growth of the island's economy. In 1753, a delegate was sent to Venice to ask that Argostoli be made the administrative capital of the island. After six years of petitioning, this request was finally granted and, in 1759, Argostoli became the capital of Kefalonia.

Before the turn of the eighteenth century, Argostoli had developed into a town of order with elegant mansions and graceful bell-towers. During the early nineteenth century, the first governor under British administration, the Swiss Philippe de Bosset (1810-1814), a colonel in the British army, carried out further improvements to the island's infrastructure. Under his governorship the many arched Drapano causeway bridge was built and he also built roads to Sami and Assos.

Colonel Sir Charles Napier, a later governor appointed in 1821, continued with road building, erected public buildings and created a public park in Argostoli which was named Napier Park. Napier was obviously at ease amongst the Greeks of Kefalonia as this entry in his diary from 1825 shows:

Now I am once more amongst the merry Greeks who are worth all other nations put together. I like to see, to hear them. I like their fun, their good humour, their paddy ways, for they are very like Irishmen. All their bad habits are Venetian. Their wit, their eloquence, their good nature are their own.

The wealthier residents of Argostoli enjoyed a high standard of living and cultural activity, enhanced by the installation of electricity in 1908. Decline came with the World Wars of the twentieth century and Greece's civil war afterwards. Before the earthquake in 1953, the town was beginning to return to a more settled existence.

Everything changed with the devastating earthquake on 12 August 1953 which completely flattened Argostoli with barely a structure left standing. Gone were most of the graceful mansions and public build-ings leaving streets piled with rubble. Many Kefalonians chose to emigrate but, with the help of other European countries, rebuilding was set in motion. Little thought was given to style initially, it being more important to rebuild homes and administrative buildings as quickly as possible. Efforts to re-establish some of its earlier style and grace, can be seen in more recent buildings like the Theatre and in the restoration of some older buildings.

Despite the loss of its former Venetian ambience, Argostoli is a friendly and thriving town with a charm of its own.

WALK ROUND THE TOWN

Start out in the area of the central square which becomes the focal point of summer evening activity in the town. Traffic is banned and Greek families come to enjoy the café atmosphere of the spacious square, where children can play in safety. Facing the square is the nondescript Town Hall building, a victim of the hurried reconstruction after the earthquake of 1953.

South from the square is the **Archaeological Museum** displaying an interesting collection of Mycenaean, Hellenistic and Roman finds from the island; much depleted now, as an earlier museum and many exhibits were destroyed in 1953. Amongst the excellent exhibits there is a fine Roman bronze head from the third century AD and, of particular appeal, a sculpted plaque and disc found in the Melissani Cave thought to be connected with the god Pan cult. It is open from Tuesday to Sunday, 9.30am-3.00pm; closed Monday and holidays. There is an admission charge.

The bright facade of the **Kefalos**

THE EARTHQUAKE OF 1953

The Kefalonians were not completely unprepared for the earthquake of 12 August 1953, only for the extent of the devastation. A couple of strong tremors during the preceding days had alerted the population to the danger and persuaded many to abandon their homes to live in the open. The strongest tremor, which registered 7.5 on the Richter scale, swept up through Zakynthos and Kefalonia. It veered off before reaching the northern tip of the island at Fiskardo, which escaped relatively unscathed. An eye-witness account tells of the rippling effect of the tremor's approach; of how he looked round to see people dancing like puppets and then suddenly found himself being tossed helplessly about.

Argostoli and much of the island were reduced to rubble. It is reckoned that eighty-five per cent of the buildings were totally demolished. Fortunately, loss of life was limited because of the warning tremors beforehand. The British were first on the scene to help the inhabitants by organizing shelters and restoring some of the infrastructure. At first, the inhabitants were suspicious of high buildings and the square, red-tile roofed bungalow type of house stems from that time. All building specifications since then, have to withstand earthquakes of well over 8 on the Richter Scale.

Earthquakes have always been a problem in this part of the world. One reason why Kefalonia has little to show of the Byzantine influence is the result of earthquakes during the seventeenth century. Damage was even inflicted in the nineteenth century which resulted in some rebuilding. In fact, between August 1953 and April 1954 a further 3,000 tremors were recorded. Minor tremors are a fact of every day life but mostly go unremarked except by visitors unused to such phenomena.

A sobering photographic record of pre- and post-earthquake Argostoli is clearly displayed in the Historical and Folklore Museum within the Korgialenios Library, which is situated on the road behind the Theatre.

Theatre draws the eye up right on leaving the Archaeological Museum. It has only recently been rebuilt after the original theatre was destroyed by German incendiaries in 1943. Founded in 1857 by public subscription, in return for which each founding member owned a box, the theatre opened its doors in 1859.

Music and drama figured highly in the cultural life of the Ionian islands as a whole and touring companies regularly came over from Italy. A production of La Traviata, with scenery painted by a stage designer from the Fenice Opera House in Venice, was presented on the opening night. The theatre was also used increasingly for dramatic works in Greek. Theatre activity is usually at its height between October and

Continued on page 40...

Top left: Main Square, Argostoli
Top right: Marina Ouzeri, Argostoli
Right: Main Square, Argostoli
Below: Argostoli Marina

EATING OUT IN ARGOSTOLI/LASSI

Good eating can be enjoyed in many resorts around the island but the selection of restaurants is particularly good in Argostoli town, which offers some of the best eating in the Ionian islands. Here are a few recommendations to start with but there are other restaurants equally good. The comparative prices are indicated by $ for cheap to $$$ for expensive.

Patsuras
Located on the sea front close to the Lixouri ferry terminal. A different selection of good Greek dishes every night, diners are invited into the kitchen to make their selection. The house wine is good too, ask for spitiko krasi. Popular with the locals. $

The Captain's Table *(right)*
On the sea front, located on the corner of the street leading to the main square. Good food from an interesting menu. $$

El Greco
Up from the main square opposite the park. Outside dining at the rear. Good selection of Greek food and pizzas. Free delivery take-away service. $

Kiani Akti
Projecting out over the water opposite the Naval Academy. Traditional Greek food with wide choice of mezedes. $$

Taverna Sirtaki
Lassi; well frequented taverna on the seaward side of the road. A good range of traditional and international dishes. $$

Monte Nero
Lassi. lying on the inland side of the Lassi road, not far from the road crossing the hill into Argostoli, this is another restaurant popular with locals and tourists alike. Traditional Greek and international cuisine. $$

the start of Lent; for current productions enquire at the Tourist Office. Head up along the left side of the Theatre to the **Korgialenios Library and Museum**.

Korgialenios Cultural and Historical Museum, situated beneath the library of the same name, was established by Mrs Eleni Kosmetatou in 1960 and opened in 1966. This enterprising lady has gathered together a superb collection of artifacts. Exhibits are kept in pristine condition and are thoughtfully displayed, with explanations in English. Exquisite examples of lace work, costumes, household utensils and tools etc. reveal the high standard of living and culture enjoyed by the wealthy inhabitants. There is also a folkloric room, a small impressive ecclesiastical display and a riveting photographic record of more recent history.

The collection is a shining example of how a museum should be laid out and interestingly presented. A definite must for visitors young or old. It is open from Monday to Saturday, 9am-2pm; closed Sunday. There is an admission charge.

The Korgialenios Library was founded in 1924 with a bequest from Marinos Korgialenios, destroyed in 1953 and since rebuilt. It houses some 46,000 volumes and historical documents relating to the history of Kefalonia. From the library, return down past the Archaeological Museum to turn right into vivid and vibrant **Lithostroto** now attractively pedestrianized.

Narrow Lithostroto was part of the first area to be built and inhabited in Argostoli and named so because it was the first street to be paved in stone. It has always been the shopping heart of town and is lined with a selection of boutiques, the post office and shops selling a range of goods, especially souvenirs. Along this street can also be found the **church of Ag Spiridon** (Corfu's patron saint). A procession leaves from here every 12th August to commemorate the 1953 earthquake. Further along is the Roman Catholic **church of Ag Nikolaos** behind which is located the 1957 **Greek Orthodox Cathedral.**

The revitalised bell-tower, on the right beyond the post office, was built by the Venetians in the eighteenth century when the small square opposite was a lively spot called the 'Piazetta'. The **Bell Tower** now houses a small café run to help the mentally impaired back into employment.

Drink with a difference

It is worth stopping at the Bell Tower just for the home-made lemonade and gastronomic intrepids might be tempted by a Submarine, described as a spoonful of chewy vanilla mastic submerged in ice-cold water! Anybody with strong legs is free to climb the four flights of near-vertical steps to the top of the tower to get a bird's-eye view of Lithostroto street and a panoramic view over Argostoli.

From here take a left turn to reach the sea front amidst a busy food shopping area, although the major supermarkets lie to the right beyond Drapano bridge, near the bus station.

At the place where you emerge there are some local supermarkets, bakers, butchers and an excellent fruit and vegetable market. The market appears to remain open all day every day in season and the produce is fresh and reasonably priced.

Along the quayside to the north fishermen sell directly to the customer, their catch, an assortment of familiar and often unusual fish, displayed for selection. Most local shopping activity takes place early morning and in the evening on late shopping days. Views stretch out beyond the lagoon to the hills on the far side, now reached across the Drapano causeway bridge that slices the lagoon into two parts.

The 1,000yd (900m) long **Drapano Bridge** was built at the instigation of the then British governor, Colonel Philippe de Bosset in 1813. This link with the coast opposite was greeted with suspicion at first, the townspeople not too happy that unruly elements in villages on the far side of the lagoon would have easier access to Argostoli. Bridge building was made easier by the shallow water at this point and the first bridge, on wooden trestles, took only fifteen days to erect.

It was replaced with one made of interlocking stones, without the use of cement, three years later and widened in 1842. It proved to be an earthquake survivor and is still in use today. The obelisk halfway across commemorates the date of the bridge and Colonel de Bosset. An alternative road now skirts the top end of the lagoon, passing close to the site of ancient Krani, but involves a moderate detour.

Palm trees and seats line the black and white pebble patterned promenade, which separates the road from the quay. At the northern end are the tourist office and the departure point for ferries to Lixouri. Beyond, the road does a 2.5 mile (4km) loop round the peninsula to the resort area of Lassi, which is actually only a fifteen minute walk over the hill from Argostoli.

A different route back to the middle of town from the Lixouri ferry port is to head inland to Leoforos Rizospaston. This wide spacious avenue lined with oleander and palm trees leads directly back to the square. Alternatively, continue along the loop road for around 0.6 miles (1km), to see one of the island's more unusual features. Away from the main holiday season the road is fairly quiet and wends along the peninsula close to the shore for most of the way.

On the shore behind a nightclub and restaurant are the **Katavothres**, swallow holes down which seawater used to disappear in volumes but not since the earthquake. Changes seem to have occurred and less water flows these days. A waterwheel is the only reminder of a nineteenth century watermill which once stood on the site and, before World War II, the water power was harnessed to fuel an electricity plant. The lighthouse at the end of the peninsula is reached in a further half a mile (1km).

The **Ag Theodori lighthouse** was constructed in 1829 under the Napier administration. A round Doric style building, it was destroyed in the earthquake of 1875 and rebuilt to the original plan. This is a good spot to enjoy watching the sun set. Either return to Argostoli by the same route or continue round the peninsula to Lassi.

A DAY IN FISKARDO

Tucked away on the northern tip of the island, Fiskardo is a picture postcard port set in a natural bay. Red-roofed pastel hued houses crowd the waterfront looking onto an azure blue bay full of dancing yachts. A table on the quayside here is all that is needed to feel at peace with the world. If there is an urge to wander then there are things to see and enjoy.

Fiskardo

Pleasures of Fiskardo:

- The charm of the quayside
- A wander around the village to see some Venetian and neoclassic pre-earthquake houses, the only ones on the island
- Inspect the old Byzantine church on the headland
- See the excavations of a Roman site showing sarcophagi
- Enjoy a swim from the small shingle beach nearby
- Visit the church of Panagia.

Fiskardo usually features on the island tours offered by tour operators but it is worth more time than a brief stop. On weekdays buses leave Argostoli bound for Fiskardo in the morning, returning late afternoon. The ferry boat from Fiskardo to Sami offers a more romantic way to travel back. The boat calls in at Ithaka but only to load and it is straight off again. Check the return bus times from Sami to Argostoli to ensure that the times dovetail.

Above & Below: Fiskardo

HISTORY OF THE VILLAGE

There was a period in history, before the advent of roads, when remote Fiskardo was popularly believed not to be part of Kefalonia but to be on an altogether different island. Perhaps it was this isolation that attracted settlers throughout the ages. These ages start very early for Fiskardo, as early as prehistoric times, and the whole area is littered with archaeological evidence in the form of flint axeheads, ridged knives and similar tools. During Mycenaean times, Fiskardo was subordinate to Sami when it was known simply as Panormos, a descriptive term meaning a 'bay for all' indicating a safe bay for shipping.

A stronghold built with massive polygonal stonework in typical Mycenaean style exists at Pyrgos, which lies in the mountains south of Fiskardo, near Plagia, and coins found there suggest occupation in Roman times. Excavations now in hand in Fiskardo itself show a burial ground from the Roman period right by the sea edge. Much of the area around Fiskardo has been declared an archaeological site, which means that no new building is permitted.

The ruins of the Byzantine church standing on the headland tell of an organized community in Byzantine times and this ruin is now unique on the island since other monuments from this period have been destroyed by the various earthquakes suffered from the seventeenth century onwards.

Kefalonia has suffered many aggressors over the centuries but one particular historical event in 1081 led to a change of name for Panormos. This is when the Normans, under Robert Guiscard, attacked the Ionian islands. Robert headed for Corfu and managed to take it while his son continued south to capture Kefalonia. When it was clear that the resistance on Kefalonia was successfully keeping his son at bay, Robert brought reinforcements and landed at Panormos. The elder Guiscard became ill with fever and died, which proved fortunate for Kefalonia as the siege was promptly aborted. Panormos was renamed Guiscardo which over the centuries changed in stages to Fiskardo.

TOUR OF THE VILLAGE

Except for traffic heading to the ferry, cars are kept out of the village and made to park a short walk from the quay, which is the heart of the village and the best place to start a tour. Expect a lively atmosphere on summer days with yachts constantly coming and going, people eating beneath the sun shades on the quayside and others browsing in the tourist shops. This you can expect to see in any seaside town on the island but the particular character of Fiskardo is provided by the pastel hued nineteenth and early twentieth century neoclassical houses which form the backdrop.

For some reason, Fiskardo escaped major damage from earthquakes that so badly affected the rest of the island. Most new houses built this century conformed to the traditional style, even before 1975 when the government decreed that Fiskardo be preserved as a traditional village. Strict building regulations to maintain this neoclassical style are now imposed. Only the older houses in the village show any Venetian elements in their design.

A stepped street at the southern corner of the port leads up to the **church of Panagia** (Holy Mother), the village's only church. Standing on this site originally was a small Byzantine church, which in 1673, was converted into a monastery. Restoration was needed after the earthquake of 1767 but the monastery continued in operation until 1911 housing up to around six nuns. The *ikonostasis* inside the church is highly ornate and worth seeing but the church is mostly kept locked so it will be necessary to enquire locally for the keyholder. Celebrations for the saint's day take place on 8 September.

Roman remains

Wandering further south around the headland leads to the small shingle beach and on the way there is a view into excavations taking place by the edge of the sea. A number of sarcophagi from the Roman period are on view, which were discovered only recently during the construction of the adjacent taverna. Other Roman remains are thought to lie in this area. The beach is just a little further on and the sparklingly clear water is very inviting.

Ferries for Ithaka or Lefkas leave from a reserved area at the north end of the port. Walking beyond here one heads onto **Fournias**, the headland where the ruins of the **Byzantine church** can be seen. There seems to be a maze of footpaths

THE MONK SEAL

The sea between Kefalonia and Ithaka is frequented by the rare and endangered monk seal, *Monachus monachus* which thrives in the warm waters of the Mediterranean and Atlantic off the coast of North Africa.

Mentioned by Homer, they were much more prolific in the ancient world but have been disturbed over recent centuries by the loss of breeding habitats and by conflict with fishermen. This rather shy animal takes refuge in caves and remote places out of sight of man to give birth to its young, usually a single pup. Tourist development along the coast and increased leisure activity around the seashores have seriously interfered with the regular haunts of this species.

The monk seal lives on fish and octopus but, with ever diminishing supplies, it has come into direct competition with fishermen. Too many times in the past has the conflict been resolved simply by killing the seal, especially when they get caught up in nets. Now the emphasis is strictly on conservation and the World Wildlife Fund supports a project to conserve a small population of these seals that is known to exist in the area around Kefalonia, Ithaka and Lefkas.

leading up to the church but with the ruins standing on the highest point and clearly in view, picking a route through presents no difficulty. There is speculation that before Christianity a temple to Apollo stood on this spot, which following the island's conversion towards the end of the first century, was replaced by a church. It is believed that this Byzantine church was built originally in the sixth century.

The most impressive parts visible today are the two towers guarding the church entrance, which illustrate the dual role of the church in troubled times as a safe refuge as well as a place of worship. Also on the headland is an engraved rock known as the **Throne of Queen Fiskardo**. This ancient place of worship is believed to be a sacrificial altar. Towards the end of Fournias headland is a Venetian lighthouse.

A DAY IN LIXOURI

Lixouri is the second largest town on Kefalonia and lies on the Paliki peninsula. Built around a port, it is a modern town with even more of a working atmosphere than Argostoli but worth a visit to absorb the atmosphere which is perhaps more Greek than anywhere else on the island.

Lixouri

Pleasures of Lixouri:

- Enjoy a ferry ride
- Explore the town
- Visit the museum of ikons
- Swim from Lepeda beach

The easiest way to get to Lixouri from Argostoli is to take the car ferry which plies back and forth to a regular timetable. It leaves hourly from Argostoli on the half hour, starting at 7.30am, and returns from Lixouri on the hour, last boat 10pm.

Lixouri is the capital of the Paliki peninsula which is the most intensely cultivated part of Kefalonia. Olives, vines, citrus fruits, strawberries, melons, figs and vegetables are amongst the regular crops and all this farming activity is reflected in the character of Lixouri. It is the produce from this area that fills the markets in Argostoli.

HISTORY OF THE TOWN

Organized settlements have been present on this peninsula from Mycenaean times and the ancient city of Pali was located on the hill just to the north of the present location of Lixouri. Little remains now to be seen of Pali since much of the stone was re-used when the town resettled. The date of resettlement is not known with certainty but Lixouri enters historical records around 1534.

The destructive earthquake of 1953 effectively demolished Lixouri, as it did many of the other places on the island. It was rebuilt on modern, clean lines with wide roads and streets well decked with trees and flowers.

Famous son

Greeting visitors at the quayside as they arrive by ferry is a statue of Andreas Laskaratus (1811-1901) dressed in long coat with top hat in hand. He was a poet and intellectual who became one of Lixouri's most famous sons.

Komboloi; toys for boys

Usually a string of wood, plastic or metal beads, *komboloi* are the Greeks' own form of worry beads, used by men to relax from the stresses and strains of everyday life. It seems to be a preserve of men, and women are rarely seen using them. Partially wrapped around the fingers, the beads are revolved in a flicking motion but there are several techniques of worrying which, for the untrained, are surprisingly difficult to imitate. *Komboloi* are thought to have developed from the Turkish rosary, which has ninety-nine pearls representing the names of Allah. This is clearly too unwieldy to use as a toy so the Greeks reduced the number to thirteen or fifteen, or sometimes seventeen. For the Greeks it is a toy or a lucky charm and has no religious significance whatsoever.

Xi beach

TOUR OF THE TOWN

Behind the quay lies the large main square which is the hub of the town in all respects. It is where the menfolk sit in shaded cafés drinking coffee, setting the world to right or simply idling away time with the help of a *komboloi*. Surrounded by tavernas and cafés, the spacious square is the place to eat in Lixouri.

The **Lixouri library and museum** is located on the coastal side, in an old mansion which survived the earthquake. The mansion originally belonged to the Lakovatos family but was donated by them to use as a museum. It now houses a valuable library of up to 20,000 books, some very old, which have been donated from various sources. Ikons and religious artifacts figure prominently in the museum section.

Nearby is the **church of Ag Haralambos,** named after the patron saint of the town. Haralambos was a priest from Asia Minor who, in AD198, survived Christian persecution. This was despite reputedly being over a hundred. His remains were kept in a monastery in Meteora and presented to the town only in 1952. The sculptured figure decorating the bell tower of the church represents the plague from which the town was protected by none other than Ag Haralambos.

Wandering to the south of town leads to a number of small shingle beaches but the best is **Lepeda** which lies 1.9 miles (3km) south of town. The simplest option is to use a taxi and arrange a time of collection. Picturesque Lepeda beach, of rich golden sand, sits within a cove bounded by a rocky outcrop to the north. On hand is a small *ouzeri* supplying drinks and snacks and there are sun beds and shades to hire.

MORE BEACHES

For those with transport or prepared to use a taxi, there are a number of other beaches to visit at the south end of the Paliki peninsula, around 5 miles (8km) south of Lixouri. The most distant is at **Akrotiri** on the southernmost tip, where a crescent of golden sand lies in a small bay, very natural and quiet. Nearby **Kounopetra** has a small port for fishing boats but nowhere to swim except from the rocks.

East of Akrotiri is **Xi** beach where Sahara red sand contrasts sharply with the putty white cliffs behind. It has seasonal tavernas and a hotel on hand but is clearly still developing. Sun beds and umbrellas can be hired on the beach. East of Xi is **Megas Lakos,** the last of the beaches on the southern coast. It offers a narrow stretch of golden sand, which extends towards and into Xi. It has a taverna and some seasonal accommodation but little else.

Further west than Akrotiri lies the curious little spot of **Ag Nikolaos** and **Vatsa Bay.** There is a small beach and a rustic café bar, which proudly features a blue toilet pedestal and umbrella as a comfortable lookout post. A creek lined with small boats runs into the bay here and a hand-propelled ferry provides access to the far bank.

Of the beaches on the Paliki peninsula, **Petani** enjoys the most spectacular setting with shades of the more famous Myrtos beach. It lies on the west coast and provides motorists with an opportunity to drive through the heart of the peninsula and explore villages that tourists seldom reach.

A TRIP TO ITHAKA

Ithaka (Ithaki in Greek and Thaki to the locals), is the fifth largest island in the Ionian group. It is almost two mountainous islands connected by a narrow neck of land and lies a few miles (kilometers) east of northern Kefalonia. Vathy, the capital, and Perahori village lie in the southern part whilst a cluster of villages in the north form the other most populated area.

This is the reputed home of the hero in Homer's *Odyssey*, Odysseus, King of Ithaka (see feature box on Odysseus). The island's barren mountains leave little space for habitation but picturesque ports and sleepy villages have gained a toehold in fertile pockets. Most of what there is to see can be visited in the course of a day trip.

Things to see on Ithaka:

- Vathy, Museum and Cathedral with fine *ikonostasis*
- Cave of the Nymphs
- Kathara Monastery and Anogi
- Pilikata Archaeological Museum
- Exogi and Platrithias hill villages
- Frikes and Kioni coastal villages

There are a number of boats daily to Ithaka from Fiskardo and Sami plus one from Ag Efimia. Check sailing times with a local shipping office or travel agent as times are liable to seasonal and yearly change.

Organized trips include a tour of the island but independent tourists with a hire car have more flexibility. Most of the ferries carry cars but always check. Foot passengers need to choose their port of entry carefully. Frikes is a small picturesque fishing village, 1.9 miles (3km) from Stavros the main village in the north of the island. There are facilities in Frikes and it is possible to walk to the surrounding villages. It is also possible to hire a taxi; ask at one of the tavernas.

Pisso Aetos is out in the middle of nowhere; a narrow strip of shingle beach and a jetty. Taxis sometimes meet the boat but not reliably so and it is a long walk to the nearest town of Vathy. Those taking their own car can make the most of the island in a day by sailing from Fiskardo to Frikes and returning from Pisso Aetos to Sami.

HISTORY OF THE ISLAND

The island was first inhabited between 4000 and 3000BC as finds displayed in the Pilikata Museum suggest. By around 1500BC the whole island was inhabited and,

49

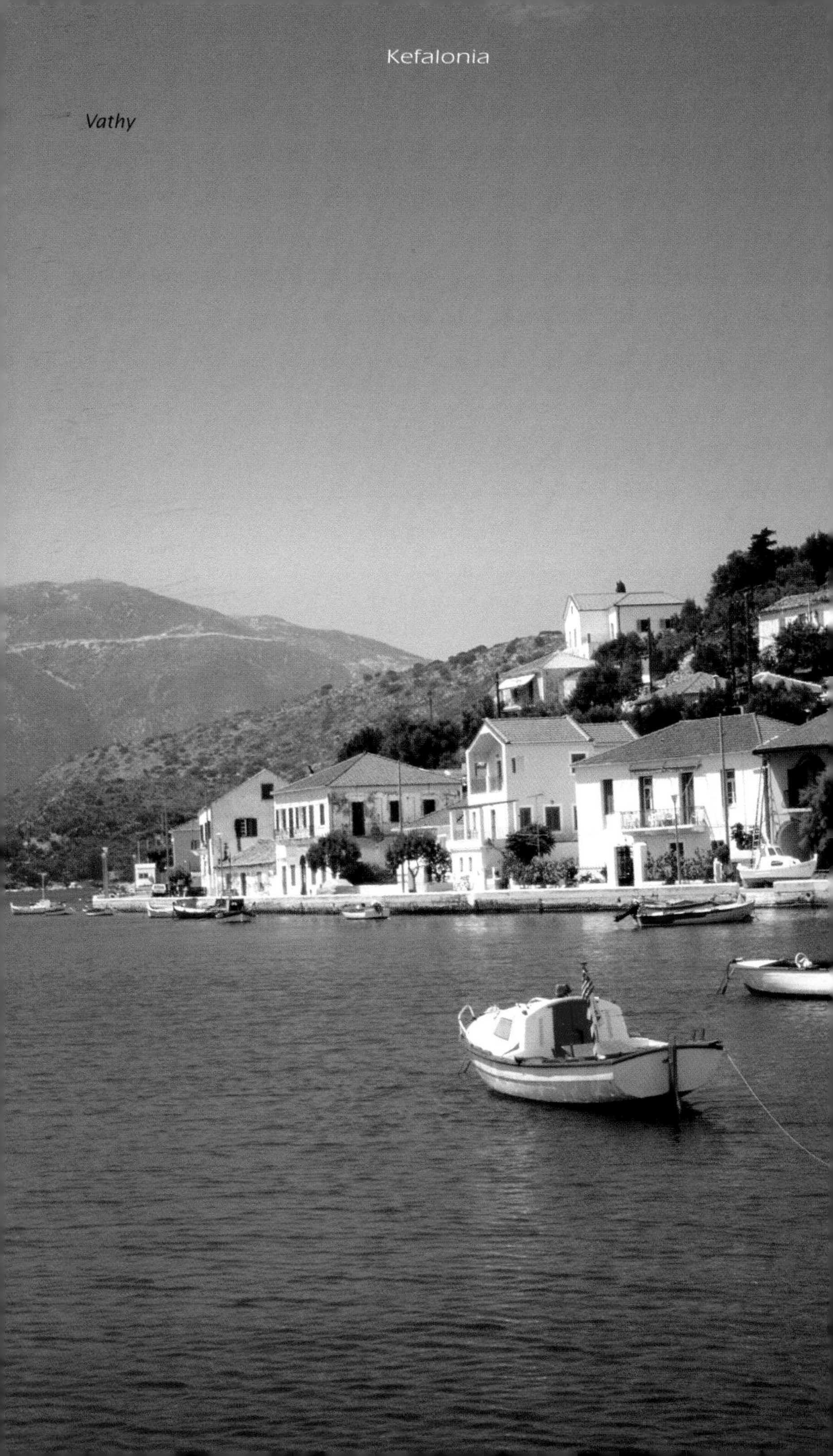

Vathy

along with Kefalonia, developed into an important Mycenaean outpost. In Homer's *Odyssey*, Ithaka is supposed to have been ruled by Odysseus around 1200BC. A later decline in population, especially in the south, is attributed to a lack of fertile soil but the north remained populated and cultivated.

The island flourished as a commercial station from 734BC, when it was on the shipping route between Corinth and its colony of Corfu. Activity was based in the north part of the island and the port town of Jerusalem, in the Bay of Polis. The town has long since vanished beneath the waves, abandoned and then finally sunk during an earthquake in AD967. During the Roman occupation Ithaka became part of the Roman province but their control crumbled after AD337 when the Roman Empire was split into two.

Under Norman rule and then the Orsini Family, Ithaka's history continued following a course similar to that of nearby Kefalonia. It was sacked by the Turks, at the end of the fifteenth century, who took hostages to sell as slaves. Many who were left fled, seriously depleting the population. When they resumed control in AD1500, the Venetians encouraged re-population of the island by offering grants of land and exemption from taxes.

In the sixteenth century Vathy became the capital of the island. Poor soil meant little cultivable land so the islanders turned to the sea for a living. By the seventeenth century, the island's fleet was being used for trade with Europe and for attacks against the Turks.

At the time of union with Greece in 1864, Ithaka had a sound reputation in commerce and shipping.

Kioni

ODYSSEUS ON ITHAKA AND KEFALONIA

Homer's *Odyssey* can arguably be described as the world's first novel complete with characters and a plot. Homer was actually a poet and a teller of myths and legends and his epic works, the *Iliad* and *Odyssey*, have become part of the literary heritage not just of Greece but of all nations of the world. The books represent two aspects of the Trojan War during the Mycenaean period that came to an abrupt end in 1100BC. The date of Homer's work is not clearly known but thought to be around 700BC so he was relating legends which had been around for some 500 years. His works, a marriage of fact and fiction, have provided a battleground for scholars over centuries striving to sort one from the other and identify fictional places with real locations.

The *Iliad* describes events in the east of the region, in what is now Turkey, but the *Odyssey* follows the travels of hero Odysseus, King of Ithaka, back home from the wars. Scholars have struggled to identify mythical places with locations in the Ionian islands, generating many claims and counter claims from the islands themselves, and they are still arguing.

Apart from our hero Odysseus (Ulysses to the Romans), the story also has a 'goody' in the form of Athena, goddess of wisdom, who carefully guides Odysseus along his precarious voyage home, and a 'baddy', Poseidon, god of the sea. Poseidon is so enraged with Odysseus that he sows nothing but disaster and torment in his path back towards his homeland and faithful wife, who spends all of her time fending off a plague of would-be suitors. Thanks to Poseidon's vindictiveness, it takes Odysseus ten years to get home from the wars although the nymph Kalypso took rather a fancy to Odysseus and kept him prisoner for seven years.

Ithaka naturally is full of references to Odysseus and Kefalonia too, mentioned as Sami by Homer, lays plenty of claims but these are mentioned in the appropriate places in the text.

Unfortunately Ithaka, like nearby Kefalonia, has suffered earthquake damage over the centuries. This, coupled with little sustainable land, has led many to emigrate, although a growth in tourism is reversing this trend and encouraging some islanders to return.

IN AND AROUND VATHY

Pisso Aetos is nothing more than a sweep of bay with a jetty. Aetos means 'eagle' in Greek. The narrow beach is used by swimmers and the jetty is shared by local fishermen and a *kantina* for drinks and snacks.

A road winds up the hill from the quayside to a saddle, the site of ancient Alalkomenes and on the hill above that of an acropolis; known locally as 'Odysseus' Castle'. There are remains of a Cyclopean wall and Hellenistic cemetery. Schliemann excavated a Mycenaean tomb here.

The citadel dates from 1400BC and was destroyed by the same earthquake that felled Delphi in 400BC. Lack of funding has led to spasmodic excavation of this site, which links to the four ancient cities on Kefalonia. A Sanctuary to Apollo, the foundations of a temple and more recently an irrigation fountain, apparently the first of its type discovered in Greece, have been revealed. Continue on over the hill to join the main road where a right turn leads to Vathy, the capital.

Watch out for a road off to the right, signposted to the **Cave of the Nymphs**, which wends for 1.5 miles (2.5km) into the countryside. Follow the signs to a small parking area below a little green hut on the hillside. A paved path leads uphill a short way to the hut and opening into the cave. The cave lies at an altitude of 623ft (190m) and is entered via an iron gate, which is usually unlocked.

Here is where Odysseus is said to have hidden gifts from Alkinoos, king of the Phaeacians who lived on Scherie (Corfu). Mere mortals enter through this northern gate whilst the gods had exclusive use of a southern entrance. Once through the narrow opening, steps lead down into a deeper pit-like cave lit by a shaft of light. Excavations here in 1805 revealed pottery, clay figurines and a marble base for a statue.

Back on the main road, continue towards Vathy past the island's main beach of **Dexia**.

Vathy (deep) is the main port and capital of Ithaka, enclosed by hills and edging the far end of the horseshoe shaped inlet. Its pastel-shaded red-tiled houses exude an air of serenity where nothing much appears to move. The small island of **Lazaretto**, at the entrance to the port, was a place of quarantine from 1668 under the Venetians and English.

Ancient landing place

Dexia is thought to be the Homeric cove of Forkis (named after the Old Man of the Sea) and the spot where the Phaeacians landed the sleeping Odysseus on his return to Ithaka.

History of Vathy

There does not appear to have been a large settlement here before the sixteenth century but, according to ancient inscriptions, there may have been a temple to Artemis and some Roman tombs have been found. When pirate activity was quashed sometime during the sixteenth century, the old capital of Paliohora in the hills was moved down to Vathy. From then on, Ithaka developed a lucrative, commercial maritime trade and began to prosper. Like Argostoli, it was a town of graceful Renaissance and neoclassical style houses before the 1953 earthquake. Rebuilding after the earthquake mainly followed the old architectural style, a decree of 1978 further protecting it from unsightly development.

After union with Greece, it was converted for use as a jail and eventually demolished by earthquakes.

In **Vathy cathedral** of 1580 is a particularly fine *ikonostasis*, carved by craftsmen from Metsovo on the mainland. The **Vathy Archaeological Museum** (open: 8.30am-2.30pm; closed Mondays and holidays) houses a collection of artifacts found on the site of ancient Alalkomenes and elsewhere on the island. It lies one block back from the sign located on the jetty.

Continue following the road around the inlet to the ruined fortress of **Loutsa**, with cannons. This and another fortress, **Kastro**, opposite were built by the French in 1805 to defend the port entrance. The road ends at Loutsa by an organized swimming beach above which sits the fortress. Out to the south of Vathy are two more reputed Homeric locations, the **Spring of Arethusa** and the **pig-pens of Eumaeus**, Odysseus' faithful swineherd.

The ruins of abandoned **Paliohora** lie close to the later village of **Perahori** in the hills behind Vathy. One time capital of the island, it nurtured a large population under the Venetians. Remains of its buildings indicate a defensive type of architecture and remnants of Byzantine frescos cling to the crumbling walls of roofless churches.

When Vathy became the capital, the villagers gradually moved down to the coast and Perahori developed around the inhabitants who chose to remain in the hills. Perahori, 984ft (300m) above sea level, lies in the hills above Vathy. This is the wine centre of Ithaka where a Wine Festival takes place at the end of August.

Frikes

Paliohora

NORTHERN ITHAKA

From Vathy, return along the main road north and keep ahead past the junction to Pisso Aetos. The road leads over the narrow Aetos isthmus and another Homeric site, that of Laertes field at **Agros Laerti**. After here the road splits, the lower route north to Stavros speeds traffic up the island via Lefki to Stavros. A road off right takes a more mountainous route to Stavros via the Kathara Monastery and village of Anogi.

Kathara Monastery stands at 1,968ft (600m) and is a good vantage point for views over the bay. The monastery is dedicated to the Panagia Kathariotissa who is the island's protectress. It has been used since the late seventeenth century and a festival is held here every 8 September. There is thought to have been a temple to Artemis or Athena on the site and Lord Byron stayed here on route from Kefalonia to Messolongi, where he was to die a few months later. The road continues to Anogi through a landscape of rocks and shrubbery with views along the eastern coast of the island.

Anogi, meaning 'at the top of the world', sits at a height of 1,640ft (500m) and is one of the island's oldest villages. The twelfth-century Byzantine Church of the Assumption of the Virgin has an *ikonostasis* with fine fifteenth- and sixteenth-century ikons. Standing apart from the church is its seventeenth-century Venetian bell-tower. Anogi was once a fortified settlement the remains of which lie above the present day village.

As with the villagers at Paliohora, the population of Anogi was much depleted, once the pirate threat was removed, as the people there relocated in Stavros and Kioni. On the outskirts of the village, tower two huge rock formations of around 26ft (8m) in height. The villagers have named one Araklis (Heracles) which looks a little like a petrified cactus. From here, the road descends to Stavros.

Stavros is the main village of northern Ithaka but is less populated than it was when founded by the villagers of Anogi and Exogi during the sixteenth century. Unlike Vathy, which developed down at sea level, the populace of Stavros chose a site above the port of Polis.

Stavros was an important crossroads between the ports of Frikes and Polis, becoming a convenient meeting point for traders from surrounding villages. A bust of the island's mythical king Odysseus in the main square is the only one of Homer's hero on the island. A narrow road off the square leads in just over half a mile (1km) down to the shingle beach and fishing port of **Polis**.

Ancient site

Polis is the suggested site of the ancient town of Jerusalem which was submerged by an earthquake in AD967 and Pilikata Hill, up to the right, yet another claimant to being the site of Odysseus' home the palace of Laertes. Finds from as early as the Neolithic era (2700BC) until Byzantine times have been found here including shards bearing Linear A script.

Loizos cave, is located in the hillside to the right, and was probably a place of worship during the Hellenistic period. Quite a few artifacts were excavated here, some dating back to prehistoric times and others from a later date which included amphorae, bronze tripods (800-700BC), used to hold vessels like amphorae, and figurines. A clay mask from around 200BC, inscribed with a dedication to Odysseus, also found in the cave points to local cult worship. These finds can be seen in the Pilikata Museum. After the end of the Hellenistic period the area remained unoccupied until the Venetians arrived.

Leave Stavros in the direction of Exogi. The **Pilikata Museum** is signposted up a narrow concrete road to the right a short distance from Stavros square (Open: 8.30am-3pm daily, closed Monday). The museum contains artifacts from the sites of Alalkomenes, Loizos Cave and the School of Homer.

Continue first to **Exogi**, meaning 'outside the world', known in early times as Stavronikion. The name of the modern village of Stavros probably derives from this. Exogi clings to the mountainside with good views of the surrounding seas. At the highest point of the hill, from where there is a superb panorama of the Ionian islands and mainland Greece, is located the old monastery of **Panagia Eleoussa**. Platrithias is reached by returning through Exogi then turning left.

Platrithias (wide furrow) is the administrative town for the clutch of villages at the top end of the island. Fertile soil, abundant water and ease of access to the ports of Frikes and Polis supported a population here from way back in early history until the Romans departed. Repopulation occurred about the same time as the founding of Vathy and Stavros, at the end of the sixteenth century. The eleventh-century Church of the Taxiarhi in the village was a monastery until the nineteenth century.

The fishing village of **Frikes**, may be Homer's port of Reithron. Once inhabited by pirates, this picturesque bay is a small enclave shared by tourists and fishermen. Deserted mills dot the landscape on the way round to the larger village of **Kioni** which spreads down the hillside to the attractive fishing port where yachts find anchorage. This was also once a pirate base that later blossomed then declined until tourism brought a revival of fortune.

Reminders of Homer

More Homeric sites lie close to Platrithias with the **Melanydrus Spring**, whose therapeutic waters are said to have supplied the School of Homer and cured Homer's blindness, and 'Penelope's Baths' which are in fact Mycenaean tombs. A nearby section of ancient wall is said to be part of the school of Homer.

CAR TOUR 1:
THE NORTHERN PENINSULA

This excursion out of Argostoli enjoys the fine coastal and mountain scenery in the northern part of the island. Two of the island's most beautiful villages are included, Assos and Fiskardo, and there are a couple of irresistible beaches too so be sure to include a swimsuit and towel. Opportunities for refreshments are limited to the two villages mentioned, otherwise pack a picnic.

Allow a full day for the tour since both Assos and Fiskardo are especially beautiful and both require time to appreciate them. Although the overall distance for the tour at 62.5 miles (100km) is not great, the twisting nature of the roads, and the scenery, operates against fast journeying. For those heading for a ferry, a straight run from Argostoli to Fiskardo takes around 1h 15min.

Leave Argostoli by crossing Drapano bridge then heading north. Mountains dominate to the right while on the left there are views over Argostoli Bay towards the Paliki peninsula. At Kardakata a road peels off left for Lixouri but it is straight ahead for Fiskardo. Also at **Angonas** is the road off

down left to the inviting looking bay of Ag Kiriaki. A shingle beach awaits with a small quay at one end and a taverna. By far the best approach by car is from the Lixouri road down through the village of Zola.

Once beyond Angonas the main road swings sharply inland following the contours of a gully. Watch here for the surfaced road off left down to spectacular Myrtos beach. Myrtos beach offers a long stretch of white sand, which slides away into an azure blue sea. The steep cliffs behind convert this bay into a sun-trap but there is a bar on hand to help maintain liquid levels and there are sun beds and umbrellas for hire. Perhaps the best view of Myrtos beach is enjoyed from the viewpoint on the main road when continuing on to Assos.

The headland jutting out into the sea seen from here is the location of **Assos** and there are fine views to absorb from the junction where the road leads down.

Photographers will want to pull off here but there are also good viewpoints along the descent road.

Assos clings and curls around the narrow neck of a peninsula and vies with Fiskardo for the title of most beautiful village on the island. There is an area for parking to the right on entering the village and another just over the narrow neck of the peninsula.

Assos suffered severe damage from the earthquake of 1953 but was rebuilt in a pleasing style with funds provided by the French, which is why the square is now called Paris. Subsequent developments are also in sympathy with the character of the village. There are shaded tables outside the tavernas on the small quayside either for taking refreshments or enjoying a meal. It is easy

Wall murals

There are some extravagant but fading wall murals to entertain near Angonas (Agonas) with the sight of a galleon in full sail or a young man helping an old lady up the stairs. These were painted by G. Lividas, a local folk artist.

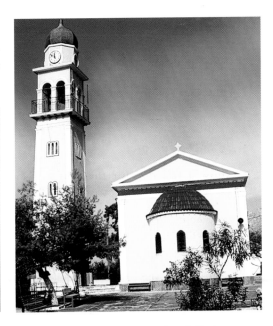

to be absorbed by its relaxed atmosphere and allow time to melt away but there are things to do including wandering up to the Venetian castle.

There is a choice of ways to reach the **castle at Assos**. A track leads up to the upper entrance and there is a footpath to the lower entrance. The footpath starts to the right of the taverna at the foot of the headland. For a round trip, walk up the track to the upper entrance, through the castle grounds to the lower entrance and return via the footpath.

Built by the Venetians towards the end of the sixteenth century, this sturdy fortress protected sixty public buildings and 200 private houses from the ravages of pirates. Even the port below was fortified. The extent of the fortifications on and around the headland, much of them still standing, is best appreciated from a viewpoint on the Fiskardo road.

Natural History Museum

Located in Davagata, the Natural History Museum may only be small but it is packed with information on the flora and fauna of the island, the geology and the marine life. There are plenty of pictures too to help with the identification of species seen around the island.

To get there from Agostoli, cross the bridge and head north towards Assos. Just past the cemetery, stay ahead for Davgata where the main road goes left for Assos. Take the left fork very shortly. Do not be tempted by the road to Davgata from the coast road which is only single track, very edgy and short on passing places.

It remained in the control of a Venetian governor appointed by the Great Council of the Republic until 1797 and afterwards it was used as a prison for a period. One of the first ruins to see when entering through the top gate is the **catholic church of St Marcos** built originally around 1604. There are other ruins still around including that of the governor's house but part of the inside is still used by the local farmers and the public are excluded.

From the upper gate it is only necessary to follow the track as it winds down through the interior of the castle to reach the lower gate. From the lower gate a good footpath descends gently around the hillside and there is a point where it closes with the upward track and is easy to cross over, if preferred.

For Fiskardo, return up to the main road and head north once again. Watch out for a viewpoint over the headland at Assos to study the extent of the castle walls. **Vasilikiades**, the next village reached, is big enough to have a petrol station but do not count on it being open at weekends. From here the route becomes less mountainous and more rural, passing through a number of small villages. Just before Fiskardo is reached, there is a left turn down a surfaced road to **Emblisi** beach, a small shingle beach lapped by sparklingly clear water.

Fiskardo is quickly reached from here and, unless heading for the ferry, it is necessary to park at the village entrance or in the car park a little further on then complete the journey on foot. For details of things to do and see in Fiskardo, see Part 3.

CAPTAIN CORELLI'S MANDOLIN

Much of the action in this emotional, funny and tragic best-selling book takes place on Kefalonia during the years of World War II. Now it has been recreated for the silver screen and, appropriately, much of the filming was done on Kefalonia.

Argostoli itself, the scene of the action, was the first dilemma faced by the film makers. The Argostoli of the 1940s no longer exists, it was all but demolished by the earthquake of 1953 and there was no room for a recreation with a realistic stage set. Spacious Sami was the beneficiary and became the setting for one of
the biggest motion pictures ever to be made in Greece. In moved the master craftsmen and with the help of a local workforce a massive stage set was built recreating old Argostoli with all its Venetian architecture.

If nothing else, it created a great stir amongst the islanders themselves and Sami became the focus of attention for much of the summer of 2000, even more so when the stars rolled up. Nicholas Cage takes the male lead role, playing the part of Captain Corelli, the gorgeous Spanish actress Penelope Cruz playing Pelagia, the doctor's daughter, while the doctor is played by the English actor
John Hurt.

Everyone would have loved the stage set to remain but the irony is that Argostoli once again was lost to the earthquake, this time a simulated earthquake since it is part of the story.

Did the film follow the book? There is nothing more irritating to readers who have enjoyed the book, maybe for a second and third time, as many have, to find the film does not follow the plot faithfully. Be prepared, there are changes in the film. People on Kefalonia who lived through those war years felt that Louis de Bernières' work gave an inaccurate portrayal of the island's occupation and these objections were listened to by the film makers. A beautiful and dramatic love story emerges but the real winner is the background scenery on Kefalonia. The ending too has changed but there are no clues here since there is no intention of spoiling the pleasure of either the film or the book for those who have not yet read the book.

On a historic note, the monument to the 9,000 Italians killed by the Germans can be conveniently visited from Argostoli. On leaving Argostoli north towards

Fanari lighthouse, take the road left up to the top of the hill. Nearby are the ruins of the old Italian garrison and a memorial shrine to Ag Barbara erected and maintained by the local Greeks.

"Captain Corelli" film set in Sami

CAR TOUR 2:
CAVES AND CRAGS

This excursion crosses to the eastern side of the island in search of adventure. The famous caves near Sami and two ancient sites are on the menu but the full itinerary includes ancient Krani, the Drogarati cave, Melissani cave, Sami, the beautiful beach of Antisamos, ancient Sami and Ag Efimia before returning by a different route to Argostoli.

Melissani cave

It is a short tour in terms of distance, around 50 miles (80km), but there are more than enough highlights to fill the day and there is at least one alluring beach impossible to ignore. A point on timing; Melissani is actually a collapsed cave containing a lake and is flooded with sunlight most effectively around midday. The best time to visit is between 11am and 1pm although it is still good outside these hours.

Leave Argostoli by crossing Drapano bridge over the bay and follow signs to Sami. Almost imme-diately the road leads through a narrow gorge over a wooden bridge. Below here is the location of the small monastery of Ag Barbara although its bell tower can be seen on the rock above. In only around 1.9 miles (3km), look on the right for a sign for **Krani** which is located just before a road branches off left to Dilinata. Turn into the track and continue for around 1.25 miles (2km) until the cyclopean walls of ancient Krani are reached. It is an open site and there is no charge for entry.

Krani was one of four ancient cities originating probably late in the Mycenaean era (1300-1100BC). As the walls testify, it was very strongly fortified in typical Mycenaean style and some of the stout walls are built with huge polygonal stones.

Said to stretch for 3 miles (5km),

Cyclopean walls

Walls of this type became dubbed cyclopean walls because subsequent generations were in awe of the enormous size of the stones used and believed that they must have been built by Cyclops, mythical one-eyed giants encountered by Odysseus in Homer's *Odyssey*.

Bottom left: Fresco in the ruined church in ancient Sami
Bottom right: Drogarati cave

the walls enclosed an area reaching down to the Koutavos Lagoon and considerable lengths of them have survived the earthquakes and still remain. Somewhere within these walls would have been an acropolis and its suggested location is to the east. The biggest threat to the walls is from the ever encroaching trees and shrubs.

Return back to the main road to continue towards Sami. A climb lies ahead before the **Omala valley** is reached, the location of the Gerassimos monastery, visited in car tour 3. Stay on the main road to wind further up the flanks of the Ainos (Enos) range before reaching the fairly high level Agrapidiaes Pass around 1,805ft (550m)altitude. The road, which branches off right at this point to climb still higher into the mountains, is explored in car tour 3. From here it is all down-hill to Sami. Look for the left turn to Drogarati before reaching Sami.

Drogarati cave is estimated to have developed over 150 million years although it was discovered only last century. As a commercial venture it has been open some thirty years. There is a charge to enter and exploration is on foot without a guide.

Over 120 steps lead down the entrance shaft to a platform which gives the first view of the stalactites and stalagmites within the illuminated cavern. Further steps lead down from the platform to a walkway circling the lowest level of the cave. Angled lighting on the best formations brings out the textures and rich hues and helps to illuminate the path around. The acoustics are good in the cave and concerts are sometimes held there. It is also cool and damp and suitable footwear is advised since the wet rock and the steps can be slippery.

After leaving the caves, a side trip is possible to see the remains of the BC 'Kastro of Sordhatos' built as a watchtower for Proni but only walls remain to be seen. Follow signs for Poros, Zervata and Digaleto then look on the right as the latter village is entered.

Otherwise, it is just a short journey from the cave into Sami where parking should present no problems.

Sami is a major port and important holiday resort set in a large sweep of bay backed by mounds of green cloaked mountains. As with other towns on the island, Sami was decimated by the 1953 earthquake and has since been rebuilt with spacious streets quite unlike the usual Greek town or village. The promenade is filled with shaded tables from the surrounding bars and tavernas and the wide streets house modern shops.

Surprisingly pristine is the port area that sees daily ferries calling and departing for Ithaka and Patras with less frequent ferries from Italy. Shingle beaches lie either side of the promenade but for the best beach drive eastwards over the mountain to **Antisamos**. It is a short 1.9 mile (3km) drive on a good road or a 45 minute walk with plenty of uphill work.

Antisamos is one of those picturesque beaches that is impossible to resist. A crescent of white shingle snuggling into green-cloaked hills shelves steeply into Homer's wine dark sea. It is a very beautiful beach and very natural but facilities are limited. Drinks are available as well as sun beds and umbrellas. There is a car park tucked away behind the beach.

The next destination in this tour is a diversion to locate the site of ancient Sami. On the return from Antisamos, turn off left towards the top of the hill following a road signposted Moni Ag Agrilion and castle. Stay ahead as the road swings left to the monastery and follow around a valley from where the walls of the ancient city can be seen on the large hilltop to the right and it is signposted 'castle'. Continue to follow the road enjoying views down over new Sami town as far as the car parking area by the ruins. The old ruins here are of **Ag Fanentes monastery** and used in its construction are many stones of the ancient acropolis of **Kyathis**. Careful excavations underway at the monastery site already reveal the extent of the buildings and the importance of this site.

Sami was perhaps the most important of the four ancient cities on the island and it remained inhabited

Ancient Sami

This is where Kyathis once stood and from here the ancient town spread down to the sea shore. Right at the bottom of this hill are the remains of a Roman villa where the bronze head was found which is now displayed in the museum in Argostoli. The walls, built originally in the Mycenaean era, are believed to have contained twenty-two entrances.

at least until Roman times. As a city state it minted its own coins, which testifies to its significance and size in that period. Homer mentions Sami as a participant in the Trojan wars and also mentions that a number of Penelope's suitors were Samians. History tells of how the inhabitants of Sami retired to their fortifications in 187BC and put up fierce resistance to the Romans withstanding battering rams and siege engines for a considerable time before they were eventually overcome.

Nearby **Ag Nikolaos** is usually locked but there is an even older ruined church with frescos tucked away out of sight below the crown of the hill. To find it, take the steps down in front of the church and head left. A canopy protects the fenced-in ruins but the old frescos that decorate the apse and its surroundings can be seen through their protective gauze covering. The canopy is currently in a state of collapse so the area is out of bounds for a close inspection until repaired.

Return to Sami and take the Ag Efimia road to head for the next port

of call, the **Melissani caves**. Action starts on reaching the village of Karavomilos which is just 1.25 miles (2km) from Sami. On the right here, hidden behind Ag Ioannis church, bounded partly by trees and shrubs is the almost round lake of **Karavomilos** which is fed from the waters of Melissani cave. From here the water discharges into Sami bay through the Katovothres channel which starts over near Argostoli. A watermill once operated here but all that remains now is the large wheel and a nearby lakeside taverna. Signs for Melissani cave are encountered a little further along the road.

Melissani cave has a collapsed roof and contains a lake. It can only be explored by boat with the help of a guide. It is believed to take its name from melissa, the honey bee. Legend has it that this cave was dry in ancient times and in contact with the earth surfaces by narrow passages which bees used quite freely to swarm in the cave. Huge stalactites made of pure honeycomb filled the cave in those days but subsequent earthquakes have changed the structure of the cave and opened access to it.

This is but one legend of many but it is certain that the cave has been around for some time, since excavations in 1963 found some interesting ceramic objects. These included three oil lamps, a sculpture of a seated Pan and a magnificent large plate with a relief sculpture of five nymphs dancing around Pan to the music of his flute. This and the other objects found are displayed in the Archaeological Museum in Argostoli. Some of these finds are believed to be from the fourth and third centuries BC.

The cave is entered by descend-

Ag Nikolaos

ing twenty steps to the landing stage, where it is necessary to await one of the small boats. Each boat takes around fifteen people and is rowed by the boatman using two oars. A trip takes around ten minutes and the boatman rows across the lake, often through a pool of sunshine, to enter a narrower channel where oars are abandoned for a time and a rope fastened along the cave wall is used instead. This section in the darker tunnel is short and then it is a reverse journey back to the landing stage.

One or two rock features that form recognizable shapes, like a chicken head, are pointed out along the way. Deep and clear, the waters of the lake are fed from the Katovothres channel which arises near Argostoli and in turn feeds the Karavomylos lake.

Continuing northwards, **Ag Efimia** is quickly reached. It is a small but attractive seaside town sitting in a deep bay with hills close by. Shops and tavernas are on hand as well as a narrow shingle beach. Nothing seems to move very quickly to disturb the sleepy, rather intimate atmosphere.

It might be hard to believe now but, before the earthquake of 1953, it was one of the island's more important trading places. Ferries run from the port here to Ithaka in high season. The town takes its name from the church of Ag Efimia, near the quay, which celebrates its name day on 11 July. On this day the town really lets its hair down with processions, festivals and dancing; it is a great day to visit.

The route back from here crosses directly to the west coast and provides an opportunity to visit Myrtos beach, if not already visited in car tour 1. For Myrtos beach turn right on reaching the Argostoli-Fiskardo road and shortly left, otherwise stay ahead at the main road and continue back to Argostoli.

Ag Efimia

CAR TOUR 3:
SAINTS GEORGE AND GERASSIMOS

N one of the car tours on the island are of any great distance and, at 47 miles (75km) nor is this. What it lacks
in distance it makes up for in highlights. Included in the tour
is the very summit, well almost, of the Ainos range, the monastery of Ag Gerassimos, a tasting at the nearby wine factory,
St George's castle, remarkable Mycenaean tombs at Mazarakata,
and, just in case a swim is in order, Avithos beach. Allow something over half a day for the tour which leaves plenty of time
for swimming.

Monastery of Ag Gerassimos

Set off from Argostoli across
Drapano bridge following signs to
Sami. Ignore Ag Gerassimos monastery on the outward journey and
save it for the return. Stay on the
Sami road climbing up the side of
the Ainos mountain to reach

Agrapidiaes Pass. Turn off right
here along the surfaced road that
leads towards the mountain top. It
climbs steadily, never dramatically,
towards the summit of the mountain
but the good road lasts until the
radar station is reached, beyond this

it reverts to track most suited to a 4wd. If the track proves to be in bad condition, do not hesitate to turn back or park and walk.

The summit area has been declared National Park largely to protect the Kefalonian fir, *Abies cephalonica*, which is the dominant tree at these higher reaches (see feature box). A short walk from the television station is a seated area from where there are superb views onto the east coast of the island. Return from here back to the monastery of Ag Gerassimos.

Ag Gerassimos is approached down a tree-lined avenue which is interrupted only by a roundabout with a huge plane tree. Visitors are greeted at the entrance to the monastery's smaller church by an impressive bell tower, which is fairly typical of the Ionian islands in architecture. Inside this highly ornate chapel, a silver casket standing near the *ikonostasis* contains the revered remains of the island's patron saint, Ag Gerassimos.

He is celebrated on two special feast days, 16 August, the anniversary of his death, and 20 October, commemorating the date his bones were removed from his tomb. The Kefalonians are joined by pilgrims from all over Greece for the celebration of these special days. Inside the chapel, an iron ladder descends into a cave where Ag Gerassimos is said to have lived for a time on his arrival.

The **Omala plain** is a fertile valley particularly good for growing grapes and it is here that one of the island's best known Robola wines is produced by Siroke. Their plant is tucked away behind the church and is open weekdays from 7am to 3pm. Turn right on approaching the large church then left onto a track immediately beyond it. Here it is possible to look around the factory if wine making is in production or otherwise simply taste wines.

A road conveniently connects Ag Gerassimos with **Travliata**, which is the next destination for St George's castle.

St George's castle is firmly woven into the history of the island. This strategic location, on a peak at an altitude of 1,050ft (320m), has probably attracted settlers from

---

Kefalonian saint

Ag Gerassimos is a fairly modern saint born in Trikala in Corinthia in 1507, son of a wealthy family. His ecclesiastical leanings were evident early in life when, in 1537, he went off to the Holy Land for twelve years and returned to take up Holy Orders. He settled in Zakynthos for a few years, living in a cave, before he came to Kefalonia and eventually settled in the Omala valley. Here, he took over an abandoned chapel to establish a nunnery and spent the remainder of his life tending the welfare of the villagers and their children. He died in 1579 and in the following years many miracles are claimed to have taken place. When his body was exhumed in 1581, it was found not to have decomposed and he was declared a saint.

THE WINES OF KEFALONIA

There are a number of wine producers on the island including Siroke Wines in Omala Valley; Gentili Wines, Minies; Divino Wines, Pessada; Sclavos Wines and Vitoratos Wines of Lixouri and Metaxas Wines at Mavrata. Only Siroke and Metaxas offer regular opening hours for wine tasting but some others may offer limited tasting days in high season.

Robola, a grape variety widely grown on the island, is used by all the wine producers in the production of their white wines. A whole raft of varieties is used by manufacturers for their red wines, which collectively are less good than the white.

Leading labels from Siroke include Robola, a light, dry slightly fruity white, Brilliante, *demi sec* white and rosé which are both very easy to drink, Melambus a fragrant white and top of the range San Gerassimos, which is made from specially selected robola grapes.

Metaxas too lead with a good dry Robola wine but have medium dry wines in the range including the white Prokis and the rosé Zefyros Breeze and red label, Arethousa Spring.

Apart from the branded wines, excellent local wine is made on the island and is as good, often better, and certainly cheaper, than the commercial variety. Much of this wine is available in the tavernas so try to ask for *krasi dopio* (local wine) or *spitiko krasi* (house wine), *yamas* (cheers!)

early times and, with the presence of Mycenaean tombs not too far away, it is tempting to believe that it has been occupied from this time. There are references to a castle there from the eleventh century but it firmly makes the history books in 1500 when a battle force of Venetians supported by the Spanish fought hard to take it from the Turks. Improvements to the castle were made shortly afterwards, in 1504, when it took the form that is seen today. It became capital of the island and remained so until 1757 when the capital transferred to Argostoli.

Most impressive are the mighty castle walls, which still stand almost intact, despite the earthquakes of the last couple of centuries and, within the extensive inner area, there are some interesting corners with ruined buildings to explore.

The Mycenaean tombs at **Mazarakata** are the next destination. From the castle, head back down to the main Argostoli road, turn left into the centre of Travliata and take a right turn towards Metaxata. Turn right down the signposted track immediately opposite the road to Pessada and the ferries. A short way along is a fenced enclosure on the right by the track. A gateway allows entrance to this large Mycenaean cemetery, which is remarkable for the variety of tombs it contains, some through shafts into the rocks.

For **Avithos** beach, return back down the track and turn right towards Metaxata. Follow the road as it sweeps around right shortly and turn left towards Kourkoumelata and Kaligata. Roads become narrower around here but signs for the holiday complex Avithos Village also lead down to Avithos beach.

Avithos, two coves separated by a rocky outcrop, offers a picturesque beach of fine golden sand backed by cliffs. Access to the beach is down steps and facilities on hand include a beach bar and taverna, sun beds and umbrellas. There are some limited water sports in the form of pedaloes and boats. It is a great place to while away the rest of the day. For a different run back to Argostoli, return through Metaxata to pick up the road via Lakithra that rides a ridge all the way back to Argostoli.

Above left: Neoclassical church at Karavados

Above right: Shrine near Ag Gerassimos

CAR TOUR 4:
SOUTHERN RESORTS

Tucked away in the south of the island are two of the island's main resorts, Skala and Poros. The road south skirts the lower contours of Mount Ainos then, once beyond Platies, descends to the intimate resort of Kato Katelios. From there it is a short hop to Skala, where lovers of sea and sand might choose to linger, and onwards via a scenic coastal road to Poros, a fairly large resort with the port area well away from the beaches.

Skala Beach

Returning to Argostoli from Poros by the inland route provides options and there is a choice to be made when the Tzanata junction is reached. A left turn leads along the high level road past the eagle monument com-memorating the resistance fighters killed by the Germans in World War II and through the 'snake' village of Markopoulo. This is the route which will be described. Turning right leads through a startling green valley heavily decked with tall Cypress trees up to Sami. From there it is back over the mountains to Argostoli.

The tour covers a distance of around 62.5 miles (100km) leaving ample time and opportunity to indulge in beach activities.

Follow the main route south out of Argostoli to Poros, which quickly leads past St George's castle to the

71

foothills of Mount Ainos. Once past the right turn down to Lourdas at Vlachata, views open up along the coast from the elevated road. Branch off right once past Platies to descend towards Kato Katelios and Skala. Would-be wine tasters should be ready to divert following signs to Metaxas winery before reaching Kato Katelios.

The atmospheric fishing village of **Kato Katelios** has a sand/shingle beach and pleasant tavernas and café/bars. It is slowly being turned into a small resort without, for the moment, losing its intimacy. Most of the new accommodation being built is scattered in a barren valley on the approach to the village.

Skala is quickly reached on leaving Kato Katelios. The present village of Skala was rebuilt at a lower level from the original after the 1953 earthquake. It exudes an altogether quieter ambience than its larger neighbour Poros with a long, long deep sandy beach, which is backed by shady pines in the middle. Watersports are also available.

Skala itself is small scale and lies out of sight of the beach, up behind the pine wood. It makes an ideal family resort, especially for younger families. There are adequate facilities with a wide choice of reasonably priced restaurants/tavernas and shops along the one main village street. At the south part of the village are the remains of a Roman Villa. The foundations have been excavated to reveal a series of rooms with their mosaics intact. These have been left *in situ* with a protective roof covering and can be viewed even if the gate is locked.

Moving on from Skala, the road follows the coastline closely in gentle undulations for most of the way. Just outside Skala, the small chapel of **Ag Georgios** sits above the shore. This was the site of a seventh-century BC temple to Apollo. A few broken Doric columns alongside the north wall of the chapel are immediately obvious but adjacent excavations show the exposed temple foundations.

The port of **Poros** is first reached where ferries connect Kefalonia with Killini in the Peloponnese. This is also thought to have been the port of ancient Proni and there are remains of walls close-by that suggest a fortified habitation of some kind. Continuing over the hill leads down into Poros itself.

Phrygana covered **Mount Atros** provides a green backcloth for the pink oleander and yellow broom which brighten the streets in early summer. A compact town, with plenty of shops and tavernas, panders to tourist needs and there is no through traffic behind the main beach. The main sweep of beach is a mix of sand and shingle lapped by inviting clear waters ideal for swimming and snorkeling. Most of the beach is backed by a spacious promenade for the exclusive use of strollers and diners. High above the town on Mount Atros, reached by a stiff climb or in a four-wheel drive vehicle, sits the island's oldest **monastery of Theotokos of Atros**.

Leave Poros by the inland route, which squeezes through a dramatic but short narrow gorge. Before Tzanata is reached, watch out for the signposted track off left that leads to the one of the largest Tholos tombs found in the region (closed Monday and at 3pm weekdays). It had been robbed out in ancient times but when it was excavated more recently, the bones of seventy-two people were uncovered. On reaching the Tzanata junction keep ahead left for the return route (or right for the scenic run via Sami).

History buffs might want to divert left on reaching Ag Georgios. A track leads round the hillside of Paleokastro and a right fork up, on a rougher track, ends at the small **Church of the Panagia**. In this locality lay the ancient city and acropolis of Proni. Little remains of the site, but those prepared to scramble around the hillside might come across remnants of walls

A striking eagle monument fills the skyline for a moment beyond the village of Pastra and a little further on, after Kremidi, a road connects down to Kato Katelios. Keep ahead soon to reach the village of **Markopoulo**.

The outward route is joined very shortly and soon, at Vlachata, a right turn offers a chance to visit **Lourdas Beach**. The road winds down through Lourdata with its huge plane tree and shaded taverna to the coast. Although this is a popular beach there is little development apart from a few tavernas and some accommodation. An enticing turquoise sea fringed by silver sand and a dramatic mountain backdrop make this an ideal spot to end the day. A typically Greek fish taverna, juts out over the sand; perfect for an evening meal and watching the sunset.

Snake festival

Every year around 15 August, the festival of Ag Maria, Markopoulo is infested with a small species of non-poisonous snake, thought to gather for breeding. This has been given a cloak of religious significance by villagers taking the snakes into the **Church of the Panagia of Langouvarda**. There, the snakes are placed on ikons and other religious artifacts and allowed to slither at will before disappearing as suddenly as they arrive. The story goes that they are nuns, who during a pirate raid, begged the Virgin to turn them into snakes. Their appearance is regarded as a sign of good luck and snake-draped locals happily pose for photographs.

WALKING ON KEFALONIA

1. Sami to Ag. Fanentes Monastery circular (4.2 miles/6.75km)

This walk ascends the steep hillside on a footpath directly behind Sami but there is plenty of shade along the way. Allow a little over 2 hours to complete the circuit.

Depart from the main square in Sami by heading up Priamon street to cross Diahion street. There are remains of a Roman baths which can be seen by diverting left briefly along Diahion street. Continue the walk by crossing Diahion street still heading towards the hill to reach a T junction in less than 2 minutes from starting out. Turn left here by the church on the lefthand corner and watch out for a walking sign on the right around a minute later and just before a wall. Turn sharp right to join a path and notice a red spot waymark. There are a number of path junctions but the main path is clearly waymarked. Watch out in around 12/13 minutes where there is a clear division of the path and both are waymarked. The right here leads up to Ag. Fanentes and the left heads to the castle which is the intended return route.

Follow the Ag. Fanentes route climbing steadily uphill until the roof of the newer Ag. Nikolaos church comes into view. The old Ag. Nikolaos with its ancient frescos is protected under a huge roof which has now become unsafe and is currently out of bounds. Head up to the modern church which lies adjacent to the excavated ruins of Ag. Fanentes monastery. The surfaced road lies just behind the ruins.

Reach the surfaced road, turn left and start walking towards the hill with the ruins of the castle. After roughly 16 minutes (see note), just before reaching a flat area to the left, turn left towards the castle. Keep up initially and gradually descend diagonally to locate a red spot. A little confusing to describe but once the path is located it is distinct. The path starts along the right hand side of a narrow valley between the hills but crosses it while still shallow. Once across, watch out for a clear division in the footpath and stay right. Eventually you rejoin the upward path and arrive back on familiar territory.

Note: to continue on to Antisamos beach, carry on a little beyond this 16 minute point and look for a blue spot on the right which marks the start of a footpath leading down to the beach

2. Patras to Katelios; about 1hour 30min.

The Poros region in the south of the island is particularly good at producing walk leaflets which are available locally This route follows the line of a number of old watermill and has plenty of interest along the way.

3. Mycenean tomb to Poros; about 3 hours

Another walk from a leaflet available at the mycenean tomb

4. Ag. Georgios (near Pastra) to Poros (7.25 miles/11.6km).

This easy track walk descends steadily from Ag. Georgios all the way to Poros and offers a good sense of space and excellent views. The route passes through the virtually deserted village of Asprogerakas, destroyed by the 1953 earthquake, although there is still some farming in the vicinity. There is an option to visit a second deserted village of Anninata. The route is shown on the Road Edition map no 304. Allow about 3 - 3 hour 30minutes.

The walk starts at the cross roads in Ag. Georgios, just 1.25 miles/2km from Pastra towards Poros. Take the concrete road heading seaward which soon reverts to track. Very soon there are excellent views over the valley to the left which stay with you for a long time. At the track junction reached after around 12 minutes, stay left (right goes up to the ancient ruins of Proni). Stay left again at the next junction, about 15 minutes later. Asprogerakas is reached a few minutes later. At the next junction reached 2 minutes later keep left again for Poros (the track ahead leads to Skala). Shortly, just beyond the church, fork left to Poros (the right here leads to the alternative higher route through the deserted village of Anninata and rejoins later).

For a change it is straight ahead at the cross road reached around 25 minutes later (the higher walking route through Anninata joins from the right). The church of Ag. Paraskevi at the diagonal crossroads here offers a good view point for looking back to ancient Proni on the hilltop. From here the steady descent continues until eventually the tarmac road leading into Poros is reached. Continue right at the fork shortly reached and follow the road past the Oceanis hotel. Around 20 minutes later, the road joining the port and Poros is reached where a left leads back into town or a right down to the port.

5. Mount Ainos by the easy route. (7.9 miles/12.6km for the return trip, easily shortened) Allow about 4-5 hours.

The road up Mount Ainos to the National Park gates is good to drive, beyond the gates really needs 4WD. Drive to the gates, leave the car and walk up to the T junction. Most of the uphill work has been done so the way is not so steep although it still climbs. This walk returns the same way so it can be shortened as desired. There is a further extension from the T junction where a left turn reaches a good viewpoint in around a further 10-15 minutes.

6. Mount Ainos the hard way

There is a real walkers route which starts much lower down, near Harakti off the Sami/Poros road. Start of on the surfaced road heading towards Mount Ainos and look on the left for the start of the waymarked route. The route becomes quite steep in the latter stages of the walk.

Fact File

GETTING THERE

The easiest way is by charter flight directly from a regional airport in the UK and there are a fair number of tour operators offering packaged holidays to the island.

For those planning to stay longer than the usual two or three weeks, it may be necessary to travel on scheduled flights from London to Athens, then from Athens to Kefalonia. Usually the journey from the UK can be accomplished in one day without the need for an overnight stop in Athens.

The scheduled route into Athens with an onward flight to Kefalonia is the only option from North America, although many Americans find it more economical to fly into London and join a packaged holiday. Flights from America to Athens may not connect up conveniently with the limited Kefalonia flights. If an overnight stop is required there is a hotel reservations desk at Athens airport.

ACCOMMODATION

Hotels:

There is a wide selection of hotels on the island spread throughout all the major resorts. The top A class hotels are situated in Fiskardo 2, Lassi 2 and Lixouri. There are more B class hotels and even more C class. Unfortunately, there is no central booking agency on the island but there is a useful web site at: www.ionion.com with hotel details but a web search for Kefalonia hotels will reveal more sites.

Villas and Apartments:

Much of the accommodation on Kefalonia falls into this category. A lot, but not all, is handled by letting agencies which place the properties with tour operators. In early season a lot of apartments stand empty and, even though they may be contracted out, it is still possible to make private arrangements on the spot, sometimes at very attractive rates.

Most of the web sites offering accommodation include rented rooms.

Camping:

Camping in areas other than on official camping grounds is not permitted in any part of the island. It is something that the Greek authorities tend to get uptight about, especially in popular tourist regions. There are two camp sites:

Argostoli Beach ☎ 27610 23487

Karavomylos Beach, Sami ☎ 26740 22480

CAR HIRE

Car hire is popular and many visitors take a car for three or four days, which is generally enough to see the various parts of the island. A current driving licence is required for EU nationals and others should have an International Driving Permit. The hirer must be over twenty-one for a car and twenty-five for a jeep or a minibus. If there is any intention to take the car on ferries, it is important to clear this with the hire company beforehand. This applies equally if you book in advance in your home country.

Cars can easily be hired on Kefalonia but sometimes a better deal can be arranged by booking and paying in advance of departure, not necessarily through a tour company but through companies like Transhire, ☎ 0870 789 8000 and fax 01923 834 919, which offer good rates and include full insurance and unlimited mileage. These companies operate through an agent on the island and usually offer rates significantly lower than those available from the agent on the spot.

When hiring from an agency on the island, check the advertised rates. These are very often the basic rates exclusive of insurance, mileage and tax. Third party insurance is compulsory under Greek law and this cost will be added to the hire charge. An additional optional insurance is collision damage waiver (CDW) and it is essential to take it. This cannot be stressed too strongly. Should you be unfortunate enough to be involved in an accident without CDW insurance and the costs cannot be recovered from a third party, then the consequences can be frightening. At best you may be faced with a huge repair bill, at worst you could end up in jail until it is fully paid. On short one- or two-day hires mileage is often limited to 62 miles (100km) per day and a rate applies for excess mileage. On top of all this is VAT at 18%.

Tyres and damage to the underside of the car are mostly excluded from the insurance cover. Take time when you are accepting the car to inspect the tyres and, if not fully satisfied, do not accept the vehicle. It is worth a moment too, to check that lights and indicators are fully operational. Greek law demands that a car must also carry a fire extinguisher, first aid kit and a warning triangle.

Motorcycles

The comments above on insurance apply also to hiring a motorcycle or moped. Insist on a crash helmet since the law says very clearly that these must be worn. Most agencies have helmets now but only produce them if they think that they are about to lose business. Make sure before you depart that the lights and indicators work. (See also Driving on Kefalonia – page 79)

Quad Bikes

Quad bikes intended for off-road use are becoming available for hire. Many are not registered for use on public roads but are being

Fact File

used by hirers for only that purpose. If you intend to hire a quad bike, make sure it has a number plate and that it and you are covered by insurance. Crash helmets too are required to comply with the law.

CHANGING MONEY

Banks are in extremely short supply outside Argostoli but there are plenty of ATM's and Exchange Bureaux around to compensate. Check that the ATM displays a full range of symbols including Cirrus and Maestro then use your normal bank card and pin number as you would at home. It is the easiest and cheapest way of obtaining cash. Exchange Bureaux take travellers' cheques/ travellers' checks but charge a commission, usually 2%, on top of the commission charged by the bank. Normally, the Bureaux are open for much longer hours than banks, sometimes extending well into the evening. Hotels also offer exchange facilities but their rates are generally less generous.

For those travelling into Kefalonia town to use banks then the opening hours are as follows: Mon-Thurs 8am-2pm, Friday 8am-1.30pm. Post Offices sometimes offer exchange facilities and are open weekdays from 7.30am-2pm, closed on Saturday and Sunday.

CONSULATES

There are no consuls on the island but the Tourist Police are empowered to issue a temporary exit in the event of a lost or stolen passport. If there is sufficient time, they will fax the Embassy in Athens to obtain a temporary passport.

Nearest foreign Embassies and Consulates are:

Australia
37 D Soutsou Street &
An Tsocha
115 21 Athens
☎ 210 6450 404

USA
Embassy-Consulate
91 Vass. Sophias Avenue
101-601 Athens
☎ 210 721 2951

Canada
4 I. Genadou Street
115 21 Athens
☎ 210 727 3400

UK
Consul
1 Ploutarhou St
106-75 Athens
☎ 210 723 6211

New Zealand
268 Kifissias Avenue
152-32 Halandri
☎ 210 687 4706

CRIME AND THEFT

On an island like Kefalonia, crime and theft levels are low and incidences of violence rare. There is no need to feel threatened in any way, even throughout the evening, but it is sensible to be cautious late at night, especially women on their own.

Many hotels have safety deposit boxes available for guests at a small charge. Otherwise, keep valuables out of sight. This is parti-cularly true if you have a car. Cameras, personal stereos and the like are best carried with you but if you need to leave them in the car make sure they are locked in the boot.

If you are unfortunate enough to suffer a loss through theft or carelessness then report it to the Tourist Police. There is a form to complete if an insurance claim is contemplated. If your loss includes a passport then you will need to contact the Tourist Police (see Consulates).

CURRENCY AND CREDIT CARDS

Greece, as a member of the Economic and Monetary Union (EMU) adopted the euro currency on January 1st, 2002. Their currency, in common with the other 11 participating countries, has notes of value 5, 10, 20, 50, 100, 200 & 500 euros. These are of a standard design throughout the EMU zone. Each euro is divided into 100 cents with coins of 1, 5, 10, 20 and 50 cents. There are also 1 and 2 euro coins. The coins have a standard design on one side and national design on the other. Both the notes and coins are legal tender throughout the EMU zone but the coins of one country might be viewed with suspicion in another.

Note: In Greece, 'cents' are called 'lepta'.

Travellers cheques, in sterling or euros, and hard currencies are freely accepted at banks, Post Offices and Exchange Bureaux. Credit cards and charge cards are also widely accepted in hotels, shops and restaurants in the main resorts. Visa cards and most bank cards can be used in ATMs.

Always take your passport when changing money. Even though the production of a passport may not be a necessary requirement, the Greeks rely on them as a means of identifi-cation. You can expect to be asked for it when purchasing an internal flight ticket. The cost of changing money in terms of commission does vary and it pays to check; normally the cheapest place is at a bank and the worst place is the hotel reception.

DRIVING ON KEFALONIA

Driving on Kefalonia is on the right hand side of the road and overtaking on the left. In the event of an accident where the driver was proven to be on the wrong side of the road, the insurance is invalidated. Unless there are signs indicating otherwise, the speed limits are as follows: built-up areas 31mph (50kph), outside built-

Fact File

up areas 50mph (80kph). Seat belts must be worn by law. The use of main beam headlights in towns and cities is forbidden as is the carrying of petrol in cans.

Unleaded petrol, *amolivthi venzini*, is freely available on Kefalonia. The grades of petrol, venzini, normally on offer are unleaded, super-unleaded and Super at 96/98 octane. Diesel is also widely available and, like petrol, is sold by the litre/liter.

Parking in Argostoli is not too much of a problem at the north end of the town but can be difficult in the central areas at busy times. It pays to observe street parking restrictions, often ignored by the Greeks, but illegal parking can result in a ticket and a hefty fine. The ticket indicates the amount of the fine and where and when to pay it. The police are not empowered to collect on the spot fines.

With one of the worst accident rates in Europe, driving in Greece demands a cautious attitude from the onset. The discipline shown by the majority of drivers in western European countries, which brings order to traffic flow, is often missing from Greek drivers but Kefalonian drivers are a little more orderly. Drive with your own safety in mind. Another major hazard is the state of the roads. Potholes are always a danger and can be encountered unexpectedly even on well-surfaced roads. A line of rocks on the road guiding you towards the middle is the usual warning of edge subsidence and there will often be no other warning signs. Minor roads, which are well surfaced, may suddenly become unsurfaced. Road works may have no hazard warning signs or irregular ones such as a pile of earth or a milk crate with a small flag.

Here is a quick check on some of the hazards frequently encountered:

- uncertain rights of way

- limited road markings

- narrow roads, sharp edges

- potholes

- ill placed road signs

- Greek drivers driving the wrong way through a one way system

- sheep, goats and donkeys

- motorcyclists without lights

- pedestrians where there are no footpaths.

Information on all aspects of motoring can be obtained from:

Automobile Association & Touring Club of Greece, ELPA
395 Messogion Ave.,
153 43 Agia Paraskevi - Athens,
Greece
☎: 210-6068869, 6068866.

In emergency dial 104.

Accidents and Legal Advice

In the event of an accident involving personal injury or damage to property, both the law and your insurance require that it is reported to the tourist police ☎ 26710 23226. ELPA offer free legal advice concerning Greek legislation on car accidents and insurance.

Breakdowns

It is a legal requirement to place a warning triangle 100yds/m behind the car. Next step is to contact the car hire agency or if the car is private, contact ELPA ☎104. ELPA has reciprocal arrangements with European motoring organizations, like the British AA.

DISABLED FACILITIES

Whilst there is an awareness of this problem, few practical steps have been taken to improve matters. As yet only international hotels provide anything like adequate facilities. Outside Argostoli, very few places have pavements and where present they are often full of trees making passage difficult in places. Ramps up and down pavements are few and far between.

ELECTRICITY

Mains electricity is supplied at 220 volts AC. Electrical equipment should be fitted with a continental two-pin plug or an appropriate adapter used. A wide selection of adapters for local plugs to interchange between two and three pin, not UK three pin, are available cheaply on the island.

EMERGENCY TELEPHONE NUMBERS

First point of contact is the tourist police ☎ 26710 23226, who should be able to offer further guidance, otherwise ring the police, ☎ 100.

GREEK TIME

Greek normal time is 2 hours ahead of GMT. The clocks advance one hour for summertime starting the last Sunday in March and ending the last Sunday in October in line with Europe.

HEALTH CARE

For minor ailments like headaches, mosquito bites or tummy upsets, head for the chemist shop, *farmakion*. If you need a further supply of prescription drugs be sure to take a copy of your prescription and the chances are that you will be able to get them, and cheaply too. Pharmacies are open during normal shop hours and most pharmacists speak English. Certain chemist shops are on a rota to provide a 24-hour service and information for the nearest

Fact File

is posted in the pharmacy window.

If it is a doctor or dentist you require, the chemist shop should again be able to assist. The island is not short of English speaking doctors and dentists.

Problems really start if hospital treatment is required. European countries have reciprocal arrangements with the Greeks for free medical treatment, subject to certain restrictions. For this reason British visitors should take an E111 form obtained from the Post Office. The story does not end there. To operate the scheme you need to find the local Greek Social Insurance office (IKA) who, after inspecting your E111, will direct you to a registered doctor or dentist. If you are in a region remote from the IKA office in Argostoli then you must pay privately for your treatment and present your bills to an IKA official before you leave the island. Up to half your costs may be refunded. The best answer is to ensure that you have adequate holiday insurance cover, although the insurer may still expect to offset some cost by use of the E111 form.

Emergency treatment, sunburn, broken bones etc., is free in state hospitals. The situation is less happy if you require treatment as an inpatient. In many of these hospitals, nursing care is restricted only to medical treatment and it is left to the family to supply general nursing care, drinks, food and even blankets. It is generally preferable to activate private medical insurance.

HEALTH HAZARDS

Stomach upsets are perhaps the most common ailment. The excessive olive oil used in cooking and over salads can be a cause of queasy stomachs so take care with oily foods, at least to start with. The digestive system adjusts to this within a few days and you can soon eat giant beans swimming in oil without fear. Squeeze plenty of fresh lemon over your food to counter the oil and, if still troubled, an acidic drink, like Coca-Cola, helps to settle things.

Drinking wine to excess can cause similar symptoms too. More serious are the upsets caused by bad water and bad food. Generally it is better to drink bottled water that is freely available and cheap in the shops and supermarkets. Avoiding food poisoning is not always possible but there are elementary precautions that can help. Many tavernas prepare cooked dishes for the lunchtime trade and these are left keeping warm until finally sold. If they are still there in the evening, and they often are, avoid them. Ask for something that will require grilling or roasting.

Care is needed on the beach to avoid stings from jelly fish and, in rocky regions, from sea urchins. If you are unlucky enough to have a brush with the latter it is important to ensure that all the spines are properly removed. Wearing beach shoes will give your feet some protection from stings of this nature. (See also Mosquitoes)

HOLIDAY INSURANCE

Whichever holiday insurance you choose, make sure that the cover for medical expenses is more than adequate. It helps too if there is an emergency 24-hour contact to take care of arrangements, including repatriation if necessary. Injuries caused whilst taking part in certain hazardous pursuits are normally excluded from medical cover. Look carefully at the specified hazardous pursuits; in recent times, injuries caused by riding a moped or motorbike have been added to the list by some insurers.

INTERNATIONAL TELEPHONE CODES

Codes from Greece are as follows:

UK and Northern Ireland	0044
United States and Canada	001
Australia	0061
New Zealand	0064

(See also telephone services)

LOST PROPERTY

This should be reported immediately to the Tourist Police, Port area, Argostoli ☎ 26710 23226 and a report obtained. It is particularly important if an insurance claim is to be made.

MAPS

The publisher Road Editions is producing excellent maps for many parts of Greece based on the Hellenic Army maps. These are the most accurate maps available to the general public and there is one for Kefalonia No. 304, 1:70,000, which can be bought on the island or in advance, at a higher price, from Stamfords in London or the Map Shop in Upton upon Severn.

Generally, road signposting is fairly good on the island with Greek signs displayed first and the Latinised version a little nearer the junction.

MOSQUITOES

Mosquitoes feed most actively at dusk and dawn but they can still be a nuisance throughout the evening and night. If you sit or dine outside in the evening, particularly near trees, either cover up your arms and legs or use insect repellent. For the hotel room, an electric machine which slowly vaporizes a pellet is very effective,

especially with the windows closed, and there are sprays available for more instant results if intruders are spotted. Anthisan anti-histamine cream is an effective calming treatment for bites, particularly if applied immediately.

MUSEUMS

There is a charge for admission except in some State or Municipal museums where entrance is often free on a Sunday during winter. Monday is now the general closing day. The museums are closed too, or open only for a short while, on certain public holidays which include 1 January, 25 March, Good Friday and Easter Monday, 1 May and 25/26 December. In addition they have half-days on Shrove Monday, Whitsunday, August 15th, October 28th and Epiphany, 6 January.

NATIONAL TOURIST OFFICES

Leaflets on Kefalonia, the Ionian Islands and general information on Greece is available before departure from the Greek National Tourist Office, addresses as follows:

UK and Ireland
4 Conduit Street
London W1R 0DJ
☎ 0207 4959 300

USA
645 Fifth Avenue
Olympic Tower 5th Floor
New York NY10022
☎ 421 5777

Australia & New Zealand
37-49 Pitt Street
Sydney, NSW 2000
☎ 9241 1663

On Kefalonia the Greek National Tourist Office is located in the port area of Argostoli, tel ☎ 26710 22248.

NEWSPAPERS & MAGAZINES

The Financial Times, most British newspapers, a selection from European countries and the Herald Tribune are usually available in virtually all areas of tourism. Mostly they are one day late. Expect a fair mark up in price. The place to look for newspapers is in the tourist shops, supermarkets and at kiosks (*periptera*) where you will see them displayed on racks or along the counter. A selection of English and European magazines is also available.

NIGHTLIFE

Kefalonia is not exactly renowned for its nightlife and the disco in Argostoli is only open at weekends. Things are livelier in the resorts where nightlife can be found in the bars, the occasional disco and in some restaurants which organize Greek dancing.

NUDISM

Topless bathing is commonplace on all public beaches on Kefalonia. Nude bathing is not acceptable on public beaches but is done with discretion on some of the more remote and secluded beaches.

PASSPORTS AND JABS

There are no visa requirements for EU citizens or other English speaking nationals USA, Australia, Canada, New Zealand for visits of up to 3 months. All that is required is a valid passport.

Certain inoculations are advisable for all travellers: hepatitis A + B, tetanus, typhoid and TB but none are mandatory for Greece.

PETS

Cats and dogs require health and rabies inoculation certificates issued by a veterinary authority in the country of origin not more than 12 months (cats 6 months) and not less than 6 days prior to arrival.

PHARMACIES

Pharmacies open Monday and Wednesday 8am-1.30pm, Tuesday, Thursday, and Friday 8am- 1.30pm and 5.30-8.30pm, Saturday 8am-1.30pm. There is also a duty rota for Pharmacies so that at least one in the vicinity is open on Saturday and Sunday. Usually a note on the door of the pharmacy details the duty chemist.

PHOTOGRAPHY

Signs which show a picture of a camera crossed out indicate a prohibited area for photography. Notices of this kind are posted near every military establishment, no matter how small or insignificant. Disregard this at your peril. The Greeks are still paranoid about security and anyone found using a camera in a prohibited zone faces unpleasant consequences. The photographer may be held in custody whilst the film is developed and inspected and at worst may stay in detention overnight. Photography with a camera mounted on a tripod is prohibited in museums as is the use of flash in some. Video cameras are often subject to a fee.

POSTAL SERVICES

Post Offices open on weekdays from 7.30am-2pm. They are closed on Saturday and Sunday.

Stamps (*grammatosima*) can be purchased at the post office, sometimes at a special counter, or at a kiosk (*periptero*). They

are also available in many shops and some of the larger hotels
but usually at a slightly increased price. An express service for
urgent letters is available.

PUBLIC TOILETS

The most usual sign is WC with figures to indicate ladies
(*gynaikon*) and gents (*andron*). Cafés provide the best hope of
toilets even though it may be necessary to purchase a drink.

PUBLIC TRANSPORT

Buses

The Ktel bus service on Kefalonia is good and offers a reliable
way to see the island. The biggest problem is that buses on
popular routes get overcrowded in season and it may be difficult
to board one at an intermediate stop.

Printed timetables are usually available from the Tourist
Office. The frequency of services is much less in winter but
builds up as the tourist season gets underway. Throughout May
the timetable changes weekly until the service reaches its
maximum frequency sometime in June, which is then held until
early September. The timetable holds equally from Monday
through to Friday. Saturday has a reduced service and there are
no buses on Sunday except in July and August.

Ktel also offers a selection of excursions in luxury air-con-
ditioned coaches with English speaking guides and at very
competitive prices. Island tours are offered twice a week from
Argostoli and Skala, weekly tours to different islands including
Ithaka, Zakynthos and Lefkas and there is also a tour to
Olympia on the Peloponnese, ☎ 26710 22 276 for details.

Taxis

Taxis are freely available in Argostoli and most tourist resorts.
Greek taxis drivers are not the most honest in the world and it
pays either to check the price before the journey, if it is for a
lengthy ride, or better still, insist that the meter be used. This
displays the cumulative fare in drachmas. The rate of charges and
surcharges are all fixed. Legitimate small surcharges are allowed
for a sizeable piece of luggage, for attending an airport or port for
the benefit of passengers, and for late night or very early morning
travel. Surcharges are permitted too at holiday times, especially
Christmas and Easter. Picking up a second fare is allowed too so
you may find yourself sharing a taxi.

SHOPPING

Regulations on opening hours have changed recently to adjust to
market needs. Different regions have their own views on this so

there is now greater confusion than ever over opening times.

Big supermarkets and department stores open:

Monday-Friday 8am-8pm.
Saturday 8am-3pm.

Other shops open:

Monday and Wednesday 8am-1.30pm.
Tuesday, Thursday and Friday 8am-1.30pm and 5.30- 8.30pm.
Saturday 8am-1.30pm.

   In tourist areas, shopping hours are much more relaxed. Tourist shops and supermarkets in particular are open all day long but butchers, bakers and the like tend to observe more restricted hours.

SPORTS AND PASTIMES

Windsurfing
Many of the small bays and coves are ideally suited to this sport and boards can be hired in most holiday resorts. Lessons for beginners are generally available too at rates that are still very reasonable.

Water-skiing & Jet skiing
Available at some of the larger resorts, as is parascending.

Scuba diving
Strictly prohibited unless in the control of a recognized diving school and only in designated areas. With so many antiquities in the waters around Greece, it is forbidden to remove anything from the seabed and infringements normally result in a prison sentence.

Tennis
Courts are mostly to be found in the better class hotels but some allow non-residents to use the facilities for a charge.

Horse riding
There are opportunities for horse riding, in Lourdas for example, but otherwise it will be necessary to enquire locally.

Sailing
This is extremely popular and most resorts have boats for hire. Yachts are available for hire in Fiskardo either with or without crews if the charterer can prove competence with a recognized proficiency certificate.

Continued on page 92...

PUBLIC HOLIDAYS

The Greek calendar overflows with red letter days; public holidays, Saints days and festivals. On public holidays, banks, shops and offices are closed although restaurants and tavernas normally stay open. Public transport is often interrupted too, reverting either to a Sunday service or to none at all. Petrol stations also close for many of the holidays.

Public holidays
The days to watch out for are;

- 1 January - New Year's Day

- 6 January - Epiphany

- 25 March - Greek Independence Day

- Monday before Lent - Clean Monday

- April - Good Friday & Easter Monday

- 1 May - May Day

- 21 May - Ionian Day, commemorating union with Greece

- Whit Monday

- 15 August - Assumption of the Blessed Virgin Mary

- 16 August - Saint Gerassimos

- 28 October - 'Ochi' Day

- 25 December - Christmas Day

- 26 December - Boxing Day

- Easter is variable and does not always coincide with Easter throughout the rest of Europe.

Name days
Name-days are one reason why the calendar is so full of celebrations. It has been a long tradition for Greeks to ignore birthdays to cel-

ebrate instead the special day of their saint, of which there are many. If you see people wandering around with cake boxes neatly tied with fancy ribbon, or bunches of flowers or unusual activity around one of the many churches, then the chances are that it is a name day. The custom is for the person celebrating to offer hospitality to friends, to neighbours and to almost anyone who will partake of a little ouzo and refreshments.

Some of the big name days to watch out for are:

• 23 April - St. George's day; all Georges everywhere celebrate their special day but in addition it is also the national day of Greece.

• 21 May - Saints Konstantinos and Eleni.

• 29 June - St. Peter and St Paul.

• 15 August - Assumption of the Blessed Virgin Mary. This is the day when millions of Marias celebrate and an important day in the religious calendar often marked by local pilgrimages or festivals.

• September 24th - is a special day for Argostoli when the icon of the Virgin Mary is paraded from Ag. Dionysos by the cemetery to Ag. Spiridon in Lithostroto street where it rests for a week before being returned.

• 8 November - for all Michaels and Gabriels.

• 6 December - the feast of St. Nicholas.

Easter
This is the biggest and most important celebration of the year. The arrival of Carnival time starts the long build up. This festival takes place throughout the three weeks before Lent and may commence as early as late January. Fancy dress is an important part of the tradition throughout the whole of Greece. It arises from the period of Turkish occupation when the Greeks were banned from conducting these celebrations. Driven under cover, festivities continued with people disguised to prevent recognition. Now it is firmly rooted into the custom and fancy dress and costumes are worn at all events. The children wander the streets in fancy dress and traditionally show defiance by wearing their disguises on the last

school day of Carnival.

All this comes to an abrupt end with a complete change of mood on 'Clean Monday' (*Kathari Deutera*), the Monday before Lent. This is a public holiday when traditionally there is a family exodus to the country to fly kites and to picnic, which mostly means heading to a taverna. Special meat-free menus are the order of the day.

It is back to the quiet life throughout Lent which is still strictly observed by many, especially in country regions. Serious preparations for Easter start on Maundy Thursday. How hens are persuaded to lay so actively for the occasion remains a mystery but shoppers are out buying eggs, not by the tens but by the hundreds. The rest of the day is spent in boiling the eggs and dying them red in the process. The red is supposed to have protective powers and the first egg dyed belongs to the Virgin.

Good Friday

Good Friday is a day of complete fast and widely observed. In tourist regions tavernas are open and life goes on as normal but in country areas it can be difficult or impossible to find food. Yellow or brown 'impure' candles are on sale everywhere ready for the evening church service. The serious mood of the day is heightened by the continual tolling of church bells. It is a day for remembering their own dead; graves are visited and wreaths are laid.

In the evening, the burial of Christ is the most moving and widely attended service in the whole of the Greek Orthodox calendar. The *Epitaphios*, the funeral bier of Christ, is at the heart of the services which start around 9 o'clock in the evening. Garlanded with fresh flowers and with a gilded canopy, the *Epitaphios* bearing the coffin of Christ is ceremoniously taken from church in dignified candlelit procession followed by silent mourners and accompanied by bands playing solemn music. The processions from all the local churches meet in the town square for a further short service. This is the most poignant moment of the evening, cafés close, tavernas close and there is not one Greek who would willingly miss it. The processions return slowly to their churches, stopping at each street corner for a short prayer.

Easter Saturday

Saturday brings an air of expectancy. For the evening service, yellow candles are replaced with white. Funereal drapes are removed in the churches and decorations of laurel and myrtle take their place. In dimly lit churches everywhere, services begin. Slowly the light intensity increases reaching full brightness at midnight when priests triumphantly chant 'Christ is risen' (*Christos anesti*). The sanctuary doors open to show that the *Epitaphios* is empty. Light from the priest's candle is passed to the congregation and that flame is rapidly passed from candle to candle until it reaches the waiting crowds outside. Fire crackers drown the ringing of the church bells as the crowd erupts in joyous celebration and greetings of '*Christos anesti*' ring out loudest of all. The crowds disperse shortly, carefully protecting their burning candle; it is a good omen to enter the home with the flame still burning and make a sooty sign of the cross on the door lintel.

Easter Day
Sunday is a day of out and out rejoicing. The big occasion of the day is roasting the lamb or goat. Charcoal fires are lit early in the morning and the spit roasting is done with loving care over some five hours with copious quantities of ouzo or retsina to help things along. All those red eggs now appear and are used in friendly competition. Each contestant taps their egg hard enough to break an opponent's but not their own.

Easter Monday has no special ceremonies or rituals and passes as any normal public holiday.

Cultural events.
Religious fairs, (*panayiria*), are commonplace in the summer months. *Panayiria* are a celebration of the name day of a particular church or monastery and usually held in the vicinity of the establishment. Celebrations are vivid, often beginning on the eve of the name day and continuing throughout the actual day. Eating, drinking and dancing are central to any celebration for the Greeks so the barbecue is certain to be in operation. When the crowds are big enough, vendors join in selling just about anything; baubles, bangles and beads.

Ag Gerassimos, the island's patron saint, is celebrated twice a year, on 16 August, the anniversary of his death, and on 20 October marking the day his body was lifted from its tomb.

A word of warning too. Each town and village has its own saint's day and sometimes, depending on the local whim and the phase of the moon, a holiday is called. This decision is often not taken until the day before so there is no way you can plan for such eventualities.

Sunbathing

Sunburn and sunstroke can easily spoil your holiday and considerable care needs to be exercised, especially in the early days.
The sun is very powerful even on a hazy day so great care is
needed in protect-ing yourself and high factor sun creams should
be used. Crawling beneath a parasol is not necessarily the full
answer since to some extent the sun's rays reflect from the sand.
Avoid, if possible, sun-bathing in the middle of the day when the
sun is at its highest and most direct. Sun creams help considerably
but, at least for the first few days, take some very light clothing to
cover up and control the exposure of your skin to the sun.
A slowly acquired tan lasts longer. Even mild sunburn can be
painful and may cause a chill feeling but if fever, vomiting or
blistering occur then professional help is essential.

TELEPHONE SERVICES

Hotels usually offer a telephone service, often from the room, but
expect to pay a premium for the convenience.

Telephone booths on the island take phone cards and these
are both convenient and economical. Cards, loaded with 100
units or more, are available often from the shop or *periptero*
nearest the booth and the cost per unit is exactly the same as
the OTE Tele-communications Office charge.

In the main holiday resorts a number of tourist agencies offer
a telephone service and often call themselves telephone
exchanges. Although sometimes convenient, they are run for
profit so expect to pay a higher rate.

SWIMMING

There is good swimming off many beaches on the island but there
is not always a system of warning flags to indicate unsafe con-
ditions. It is absolutely essential to use common sense when
the sea is rough or strong currents are flowing and avoid taking
unnecessary risks.

TIPPING

There are no hard and fast rules on tipping, especially since bills
by law already include a 17% service charge. Normally, the
Greeks simply leave behind the small change after a meal and
perhaps the best guide is to reward only for good service in a
restaurant. Taxi drivers expect a tip as does the chambermaid in
the hotel otherwise it is entirely by discretion.

WATER

Sources of drinking water vary on the island but it is safe for
cleaning teeth. It is advisable to drink only bottled water, which is
freely available.

Index

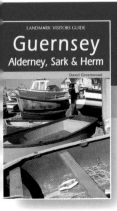

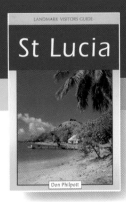

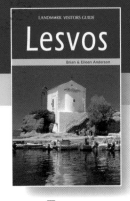

UK   World   Europe

- Riga & its beaches, Latvia (2nd edition) *1-84306-096-5, £9.95*
- Shakespeare Country & the Cotswolds (2nd Edition) *1-84306-002-7, £10.95*
- Somerset (2nd edition) *1-84306-117-1, £9.95*
- St Lucia (4th Editon) *1-84306-099-X, £6.95*
- The National Forest *1-84306-106-6, £5.95*
- Vendée *1-901522-76-8, £7.95*
- Virgin Islands, US & British (2nd Editon) *1-84306-036-1, £11.95*
- Yorkshire Dales & Moors *1-901522-41-5, £10.95*
- Zakinthos (2nd Edition) *1-84306-024-8, £7.50*

Prices subject to change

LANDMARK VISITORS GUIDE
Zakynthos
(Zante)
Brian & Eileen Anderson

Landmark Publishing Ltd

Ashbourne Hall, Cokayne Ave,
Ashbourne, Derbyshire,
DE6 1EJ England
Tel 01335 347349
Fax 01335 347303
e-mail landmark@clara.net
www.landmarkpublishing.co.uk

Published in the UK by
Landmark Publishing Ltd,
Ashbourne Hall, Cokayne Ave, Ashbourne, Derbyshire DE6 1EJ England
Tel: (01335) 347349 Fax: (01335) 347303
e-mail: landmark@clara.net
website: www.landmarkpublishing.co.uk

3rd Edition
ISBN: 1-84306-176-7

Print: Gutenberg Press Ltd, Malta
Design & Cartography: James Allsopp
Editor: Kay Coulson

Front cover: Assos
Back cover, top: Fiskardo
Back cover, bottom: Fiskardo

Picture Credits:

All photographs are supplied by the authors.
Except page 61: Captain Corelli film set – Poly Antonatos
(Auto Europe Car Rental, Lassi, Kefalonia)

Acknowledgements:

Thanks to Nick and Vivian Sklavounakis of Vivian Villa, Argostoli,
(tel: 0030 26710 23396, email: villaviv@otenet.gr) for their continued support and sharing with us their knowledge of the island.